£11·99

c'

Roles and responsibilities
in the primary school

Roles and responsibilities in the primary school

Changing demands, changing practices

Rosemary Webb and Graham Vulliamy

Open University Press
Buckingham · Philadelphia

Open University Press
Celtic Court
22 Ballmoor
Buckingham
MK18 1XW

and
1900 Frost Road, Suite 101
Bristol, PA 19007, USA

First Published 1996

A catalogue record of this book is available from the British Library

ISBN   0 335 19472 9 (pb)   0 335 19473 7 (hb)

Library of Congress Cataloging-in-Publication Data
Webb, Rosemary.
     Roles and responsibilities in the primary school: changing demands,
changing practices/by Rosemary Webb and Graham Vulliamy.
       p.   cm.
     Includes bibliographical references and indexes.
     ISBN 0-335-19473-7   ISBN 0-335-19472-9 (pbk)
     1. Education, Elementary – Great Britain – Curricula. 2. Education and
state – Great Britain. 3. School management and organization – Great Britain.
4. Teaching – Great Britain. 5. Action research in education – Great Britain.
6. Educational surveys – Great Britain.   I. Vulliamy, Graham.   II. Title.
LB1564.G7W42   1996   95-34487
372.19′0941–dc20   CIP

Typeset by Type Study, Scarborough
Printed in Great Britain by Biddles Ltd, Guildford and King's Lynn

Contents

Acknowledgements

We are extremely grateful to the 13 local education authorities and the 50 schools who participated in our research and made this book possible. We are particularly indebted to the headteachers who made us welcome in their schools and frequently gave up time, not only to talk to us themselves, but also to take classes in order that we could talk to classteachers. Our special thanks go to those teachers in whose classrooms we carried out lesson observations.

We were assisted in the fieldwork by Sheila Sudworth, who researched nine of the schools, and by five members of the Centre for Primary Education at the University of Manchester, who each researched one school, in the first phase of the project. We have also benefited from the encouragement and administrative support provided by the Department of Educational Studies at the University of York.

We would like to thank the Association of Teachers and Lecturers (ATL) not only for their financial support for the research, but also for their assistance in supplying information and for their continuing interest in work emanating from the project.

Finally, we are grateful to those organizations and journals who have given us permission to build upon material here which has been published elsewhere. These include:

ATL for material first published in the two reports of the project (*Eating the Elephant Bit by Bit, The National Curriculum at Key Stage 2*, London, ATL, 1993 and *After the Deluge: Changing Roles and Responsibilities in the Primary School*, London, ATL, 1994).

Carfax and *Educational Review* for material in Chapters 3 and 6 (published as 'The implementation of the National Curriculum in small primary schools', *Educational Review*, 47 (1): 25–41, 1995).

Routledge and *The Curriculum Journal* for material in Chapter 4 (published as 'The changing role of the primary school curriculum co-ordinator', *The Curriculum Journal*, 6 (1): 29–45, 1995).

Carfax and *School Organisation* for material in Chapter 5 (published as 'The changing role of the primary school deputy headteacher', *School Organisation*, 15 (1): 49–59, 1995).

The Primary Schools Research and Development Group and *Education 3–13* for material in Chapter 6 (published as 'Headteachers as social workers: The hidden side of parental involvement in the primary school', *Education 3–13*, forthcoming).

The British Educational Management and Administration Society and *Educational Management and Administration* for material in Chapter 6 (published as 'The changing role of the primary school headteacher', *Educational Management and Administration*, forthcoming).

Abbreviations

AMMA	Assistant Masters and Mistresses Association (now ATL)
AT	attainment target
ATL	Association of Teachers and Lecturers (formerly AMMA)
BEd	Bachelor of Education
CACE	Central Advisory Council for Education
DES	Department of Education and Science (now DFEE)
DFE	Department for Education (formerly the DES and now the DFEE)
DFEE	Department for Education and Employment
ERA	Education Reform Act
ESG	Educational Support Grant
GEST	Grants for Education, Support and Training
HMI	Her Majesty's Inspectorate of Schools
ILEA	Inner London Education Authority
INSET	in-service education and training
IT	information technology
KS	key stage (as in KS1, KS2)
LEA	local education authority
LMS	local management of schools
NCC	National Curriculum Council
NGC	National Governors Council
NSG	non-statutory guidance
NTA	non-teaching assistant
OFSTED	Office for Standards in Education
ORACLE	Observational Research and Classroom Learning Evaluation

PACE	Primary Assessment Curriculum and Experience
PE	physical education
PNP	Primary Needs Project
PoS	programme of study
PRINDEP	Primary Needs Independent Evaluation Project
RE	religious education
RoA	record of achievement
SATs	Standard Assessment Tasks
SCAA	School Curriculum and Assessment Authority
SEAC	School Examinations and Assessment Council
SEN	special educational needs
SoA	Statement of Attainment
STA	special teaching assistant
STAR	Student Teacher Achievement Ratio
TA	Teacher Assessment
TES	*Times Educational Supplement*
TGAT	Task Group on Assessment and Testing

Introduction and methodology

> Now it's a different day and a different age from when I was first
> doing this. It was exhilarating, we had the time. Dare I say it? – I
> think staff had the enthusiasm. I think that they felt more
> appreciated. Some of the things we did, like taking Romans as a
> loose theme and looking at areas of their life – like their cooking
> theories and what have you – I think education was fun in those
> days.

These are the words of a middle school headteacher who compared with
some sadness the current educational climate and its effect on teachers'
morale with that of the past when she was a classteacher. Our purpose in
this book is first and foremost to portray teachers' work as it is currently
experienced in primary schools in the post-Education Reform Act (ERA)
context. We report their perspectives on the changes and find out from
them what they believe teaching has lost and gained. In so doing we
document the diverse ways in which schools are coping with the
continual pressure for change and what is involved in managing the
implementation of successive new government directives. The titles of
the book's chapters are indicative of the potentially wide ranging and all
pervasive nature of these changes.

The book is based on the findings resulting from two phases of
qualitative research commissioned by the Association of Teachers and
Lecturers (ATL). The first focused on the implementation of the National
Curriculum at key stage 2 (KS2) in England and Wales. The aims were to
collect teachers' perspectives on the National Curriculum at KS2, to
discover how the curriculum was being planned and implemented and to
identify consequent benefits and problems. Drawing on the work of the
first phase the second examined the impact of the National Curriculum,

in combination with the other changes brought about by the 1988 Education Reform Act, on the roles and responsibilities of classteachers, curriculum coordinators, deputy headteachers and headteachers. While in the largest schools these roles were to a certain degree separate and distinct, in small schools they were all encompassed within the work of the headteacher. The fieldwork was conducted between October 1992 and February 1994 in a sample of 50 schools in England and Wales. An account of our research methodology follows this introduction.

Through this book, we hope to gain a wider audience for the teachers' voices and their actions presented in the two reports written for ATL. We also wanted the opportunity created by writing the chapters to reflect more deeply on what we had seen and what the teachers had told us in order to derive additional meaning from the data and to explore further the implications for primary education. Qualitative school-focused research can be of considerable assistance to schools and to individual teachers as a resource for reviewing and developing their policies and practice. Therefore it is also our intention that by drawing on the wealth of ideas and successful practices shared with us by teachers in the study, this book should be of practical use to schools.

We envisage three main ways in which this intention might be realized. First, schools can compare their rate of progress with those of the sample schools and locate their position within a wider framework, for like themselves the schools in the research had different priorities and therefore different rates of development in relation to the many demands made upon them. Second, teachers can reflect on their own practice in the light of the experiences and opinions of teachers portrayed in the research and weigh up the advantages and disadvantages of alternative approaches to a range of current issues such as curriculum organization, classroom management and the delegation of curriculum leadership. Third, through lists of suggestions on some of the newest responsibilities, such as organizing in-service education and training (INSET) days, they might identify ways forward. We also use our research findings to challenge some of the orthodoxies to be found in prior academic research, in management texts and in government inspired central directives from organizations such as the School Curriculum and Assessment Authority (SCAA) and the Office for Standards in Education (OFSTED). The research presents an account of what is (albeit at a particular point in time), as opposed to official versions of what should be, and provides teachers with a wider picture of how colleagues in other schools and LEAs are thinking and acting. We hope that this will encourage them to have confidence in their own judgements as to which aspects of the reforms to resist, which to reinterpret creatively to fit in with their own situation and which to implement wholeheartedly because they appear to have much to offer both pupils and the school as a whole.

Chapter 1 provides a context for the research by reviewing political and legislative changes resulting from the 1988 Education Reform Act and subsequent Education Acts in order to highlight the key issues facing primary education today. Those for whom these changes are all too familiar might want to bypass this chapter and move straight to the research findings. We devote two chapters (2 and 3) to the changing role of the classteacher. The demands of the National Curriculum and assessment, together with recommendations from OFSTED, have not only put pressures on teachers to make changes in their classrooms (the focus of Chapter 2), but have also challenged established approaches to curriculum organization and led to an exponential expansion of their responsibilities beyond the classroom, especially in relation to curriculum planning and subject expertise (the focus of Chapter 3). Key aspects of this expanding role are the greater responsibilities given to, and the enhanced expectations for, the role of the curriculum coordinator within primary schools, which form the subject of Chapter 4. Chapters 5 and 6 discuss the impact of recent government reforms on the roles of the deputy headteacher and the headteacher respectively and reveal how these two roles have become increasingly interdependent. The book concludes in Chapter 7 with a consideration of the mechanisms for the management of whole school change brought about by recent reforms and the implications of the cumulative impact of these on the culture of primary schooling.

Research methodology

Given the research aims stated earlier, two possible research strategies were considered. The first was a combination of a national survey, involving sending a questionnaire to a representative sample of schools with KS2 pupils throughout England and Wales, supplemented by interviews in a few such schools. This is a commonly used research strategy, especially for policy-oriented studies, and has the benefit of providing statistical data for a national sample, with the possibility of such a quantitative approach being supplemented to some extent by qualitative interview data in the text of a report. The second possible research strategy was a qualitative one where the intention would be to provide an in-depth analysis of the key issues within a smaller sample of schools. Since we chose to adopt the second of these broad research strategies, we will briefly explain our reasons for doing so.

Earlier research on the implementation of the National Curriculum in primary schools (Webb 1993b) had suggested that a questionnaire survey would be inappropriate for a number of reasons. First, it was clear that much of the language that would be necessary in such a questionnaire –

such as 'topic work', 'integrated day', 'group work' or 'setting' – was either ambiguous or used in totally different ways in different schools. Second, the complexity of curricular organization and planning in various schools was such that researchers could only comprehend it if given the opportunities for detailed questioning about such approaches, referring to documents *in situ* with teachers themselves. Third, examples of the 'broad brush' approach, as represented by national questionnaire surveys by researchers or by the accumulation of school visits by teams of HMI or OFSTED inspectors, were already available. Whilst these had identified general trends, such as the move towards more subject-focused topic work (see, for example, OFSTED 1993a), we felt that a more in-depth analysis of the reasons for, and implications of, such trends was required.

Qualitative research studies in education are now accepted by researchers and policy makers alike as having the potential for providing an in-depth analysis of key issues and of leading to a reconceptualization of the parameters of academic and political debate by questioning the taken-for-granted assumptions often to be found in more generalized research and analysis (Finch 1986; Vulliamy *et al.* 1990). At the same time, it is recognized that an important limitation of qualitative research, especially for policy makers, is the potential lack of representativeness to be found in the conventional ethnographic study of one, or at most two or three, schools within a single research project. Our research strategy, therefore, was guided by a combination of the use of qualitative research techniques – notably, tape-recorded interviews, classroom observation and the analysis of school and teacher documentation – with a sample of schools large enough to be likely to reflect the range of approaches to curriculum organization at KS2. Detailed accounts of the methods used in the research (including copies of interview schedules) are available elsewhere (Webb 1993a: 3–5, 88–99; Webb 1994: 1–4, 82–4); here we provide a briefer account to enable readers to assess the strengths and weaknesses of the findings reported in this book.

Thirteen local education authorities (LEAs) (chosen to reflect a variety in terms of their size and inner city/urban/rural nature) agreed to participate in the project: seven from the northeast of England; two from the Home Counties; two from the Midlands; one from the southwest and one from Wales. Either one or more LEA advisers/inspectors were interviewed from each of these – usually the senior primary adviser supplemented in some LEAs by relevant subject or INSET advisers or advisory teachers. These interviews were all tape-recorded and were based upon a semi-structured interview schedule. In addition, LEA documentation on aspects of KS2 curriculum organization, planning and assessment was analysed.

Schools were selected on the basis of personal contacts (10), from information given in the Primary Schools Directory and other published sources (12), following participation in an earlier research project (Webb 1993b) on the implementation of the National Curriculum (11), and from LEAs' suggestions of schools which they felt were either closely following LEA guidelines or were organizing the curriculum in ways strongly approved by the LEA (17). Our aim in this LEA-nominated subsample was to ensure that we had some examples of perceived 'good practice'. Headteachers were written to and/or phoned to request permission to include their schools in the project. This was granted in all but six cases, where headteachers stated that they and/or their teachers were under too much stress to participate in the research. A consequence of this may be that the research sample does not represent those schools throughout England and Wales who recognized that they were really struggling with the implementation of the National Curriculum.

This, therefore, gave a total sample of 50 schools from which data have been used for this project. Our primary concern in selecting this sample was to ensure that it reflected the full diversity of KS2 provision within England and Wales in terms of size and type of school. Table I.1 compares the nature of our sample by size of school with the 1991 figures for KS2 schools in England. It can be seen that, whilst the proportions of small schools are very similar (the smallest school in our sample had 25 pupils), our sample has a higher proportion of large schools (the largest having 668 pupils). This arose from a deliberate decision to include a higher proportion of larger schools, following the government's pronouncements that they wished to encourage the wider spread of organizational strategies, such as specialist subject teaching and setting by ability, which were thought to be more commonly associated with large schools than with smaller ones. Table I.2 indicates the nature of the sample by type of school. Given these parameters of the sample by size and type of school, we tried to ensure that other aspects of the diversity of primary schooling were reflected, giving, for example, a mix of inner-city, suburban and rural schools, a multicultural mix (from all-white schools through to one school with 98 per cent ethnic minority pupils) and a mix of religious denominations (including Church of England, Roman Catholic and Methodist). While the individual schools researched may not be representative of others with similar characteristics, we believed that a sample of 50 schools chosen in this manner should ensure that the main issues and approaches to the implementation of the National Curriculum at KS2 were identified.

Data from each of the 50 schools were collected during a day visit in the first phase of the fieldwork (September 1992–March 1993). The most common pattern for such visits involved:

- completing a school data sheet containing factual information about the school;

Table I.1   Research sample by size of school compared with 1991 KS2 schools

	Small schools 0–100 pupils	Medium schools 101–300 pupils	Large schools 301+ pupils
Research sample (N = 50)	18% (N = 9)	54% (N = 27)	28% (N = 14)
English KS2 schools in 1991	20%	62%	17%

Source: DES 1991b: 134

Table I.2   Research sample by type of school

Primary	Junior	Middle	First
70% (N = 35)	16% (N = 8)	10% (N = 5)	4% (N = 2)

- collecting samples of planning and record keeping documents at whole school, year group and classroom levels;
- tape-recorded semi-structured interviews with the headteacher and, if possible, with the deputy headteacher or a subject coordinator;
- observation of a KS2 class for a lesson;
- an interview, tape-recorded if possible, with the teacher of the class observed;
- informal conversations with teachers at breaks and lunchtime and observation, where possible, of other school activities such as assemblies.

The total numbers of tape-recorded interviews from the 50 schools in this first phase of the research were: 47 headteachers; 19 deputy head-teachers; and 29 classteachers and/or subject coordinators. All the tape-recorded interviews (averaging about 40 minutes) were transcribed in whole or in part in order that a qualitative analysis of teachers' and LEA perspectives could be made. This analysis was conducted jointly in a manner similar to that discussed in a more detailed account of the analytic procedures we used in an earlier research project (Vulliamy and Webb 1992: 216–22) using a combination of short analytic memos (Elliott 1991) written on the transcripts and a process of category generation and saturation based upon the 'constant comparison' method advocated by Glaser and Strauss (1967). Our aim has been faithfully to ground our analysis in the lived experiences of teachers.

The analyses of data from the classroom observations were both less reliable and less valid. This is because, first, they were based on more open-ended observations and, second, observation of just one lesson may well have been unrepresentative of the totality of that teacher's lessons (although it is worth noting here that, whilst in some cases classteachers knew of our visit to observe a particular class in advance at some point during the day, in others they did not). The original intention for such classroom observation was simply to provide a context for the classteacher interviews and also to use such observations to provoke questions concerning the relationships between whole school planning and classroom practice. Nevertheless, such caveats notwithstanding, we used analysis of such classroom observations: first, to look at relationships between curriculum organization and classroom organization and to consider our findings in relation to exhortations for more whole class teaching (to be found, for example, in Alexander *et al*. 1992 and in OFSTED 1993a); second, to identify the range of ways in which the National Curriculum was being taught; and third, to explore topical classroom issues, such as differentiation.

Data collection for a second stage of the research was carried out between November 1993 and February 1994 in a 25 per cent sample of the original schools, chosen in such a way as to reflect closely the earlier distribution of schools by size and by type, and located in five of the 13 LEAs. There were three main purposes underlying the return to a sample of the original schools. First, following the analysis of the earlier interviews, new interview schedules could be focused on emerging issues concerning the changing roles and responsibilities of headteachers, deputy headteachers and subject coordinators. Second, revisiting some of the schools a year later facilitated a longitudinal dimension to the research, whereby, for example, the outcome of school initiatives being undertaken at the time of the first interviews could be discussed a year later. Finally, the continuing pace of change in primary schools during 1993, associated in particular with the outcome of the Dearing reports (1993a; 1993b), was such that fresh insights could be gained into teachers' work. In stage two of the research tape-recorded interviews were conducted with each of the headteachers of the 12 schools and with eight deputy headteachers (two from the same school). In order to understand the range of activities undertaken by a headteacher, we also asked heads to talk us through the events of the week prior to their interview, using their personal diary entries as prompts. Fieldnotes and interview transcripts were added to the database from stage one of the research and were analysed using the same qualitative data analysis techniques.

Throughout this book, where it is relevant to the issues discussed, we have included the numbers of pupils in a school when presenting data; in other cases pupil numbers have been excluded, either because school size is immaterial or because we have wished to preserve school and teacher anonymity fully (for the same reason pseudonyms are used throughout).

one

The changing context of primary education

The requirements of the Education Reform Act (ERA) and subsequent Education Acts have had, and are continuing to have, a fundamental impact on primary schooling in England and Wales. While in terms of classroom practice there are still immensely strong continuities between the present and the past (Alexander 1993), the ways in which primary schools in the 1990s are managed, plan and assess their curriculum, relate to their community, evaluate their work and are held accountable for it are in many ways very different from their counterparts in the 1980s. Most of the major changes which are responsible for these differences were either set in motion, or strengthened further, by the ERA.

A dominant theme in the book is the implementation of the National Curriculum and its associated assessment arrangements at KS2 and the impact of these on the work and practice of primary school teachers. Thus in the first part of the chapter we outline the introduction of the National Curriculum and national assessment and teachers' initial reactions to it. We then proceed to give a more detailed description of related events which occurred during the life of our research project. These not only provided the backdrop to the research but also influenced the direction of the research and shaped the nature of the data collected. Throughout the book we depict tensions in teachers' commitments which are created by administrative and managerial demands in competition with those of curriculum development and teaching. Consequently, the rest of the chapter considers in turn the significant changes which have brought this about. These changes – in relation to governors, local management of schools (LMS), parents as consumers and the introduction of quality assurance mechanisms – were found to be both transforming teachers' work and having a fundamental impact on the culture of primary schools.

The introduction of the National Curriculum

The events leading to the inclusion of the introduction of the National Curriculum into the Education Reform Act have been well documented (see, for example, Aldrich 1988; Maclure 1988; Ball 1990c; Kelly 1990; Chitty 1993). Initially the National Curriculum for primary schools consisted of:

- nine subjects including three core subjects and six other foundation subjects;
- programmes of study setting out the knowledge and skills to be taught;
- attainment targets divided into 10 levels;
- statements of attainment setting the learning objectives for each level.

From the outset, the proposed orders came in for a wide range of criticism from educationalists, for example, for having a poor philosophical base (O'Hear and White 1991), for allowing no time or space for cross-curricular themes (Hargreaves 1989), for being orientated to the past (Ball 1990b), for taking insufficient account of issues of equal opportunities (Burton and Weiner 1990) and for disregarding the distinctive character of primary schools, including their thematic approach to the curriculum, for which they were once internationally renowned (Brehony 1990). Shortly after the passing of the ERA, a working party – the 'Interim Primary Committee' – was set up by the National Curriculum Council (NCC). Its remit was to draft a report suggesting strategies by which primary schools might meet the demands of the subject based National Curriculum. However, as documented by Galton (1995), one of its members, after almost a year the committee's work was brought to an abrupt halt owing to the current Secretary of State Kenneth Baker's request for the report immediately. It was then hastily drafted by senior NCC officers. The general feeling of the Committee, which was then disbanded, 'was one of disappointment and a sense of an opportunity lost' (p. 27) and the resultant 'overall blandness' of the advice – *A Framework for the Primary Curriculum* (NCC 1989) – meant that it made little impact in the press or in the schools (p. 29).

The implementation of the National Curriculum began with the introduction of mathematics, science and English at key stage 1 (KS1) in 1989. The principle of a National Curriculum and its statutory entitlement for all pupils was generally welcomed in primary schools in its initial stages (NCC 1990b; Campbell *et al.* 1991; Osborn and Pollard 1991). Teachers in KS1 reported that they found it helpful to have a structure within which to work and felt that their professionalism had increased through the process of whole school review and planning that the National Curriculum had generated. While there was concern that the amount of factual knowledge to be covered could lead to an overemphasis on didactic teaching, the requirements of the programmes of study for investigative work in science, using and applying mathematics and speaking and listening in English were viewed as likely to extend teachers' repertoires of teaching methods and provide pupils with increased opportunities to discuss, solve problems and to work collaboratively (Vulliamy and Webb 1993).

However, even during the first year, teachers found the pace and pressure of the reforms stressful and were working unreasonably long hours to cope with the preparation and in-service training (see Campbell and Neill 1990). In 1990 technology was introduced into KS1 and into KS2 along with the core subjects. History and geography were introduced in both key stages in 1991 and the total picture of the National Curriculum in primary schools finally emerged in April 1992 with the publication of the orders for art, music and PE. From the inception of the National Curriculum there was criticism of the way in which the subjects were developed by subject working parties in isolation from one another and the piecemeal way in which the orders were introduced. For primary school teachers this meant that they were expected to plan for the whole curriculum, starting from a few of the parts with little conception of the whole – like working on a jigsaw with little idea of the picture it is supposed to represent. Not surprisingly this led to problems, such as an overemphasis on science within topic work, which unbalanced the primary curriculum across both key stages.

As the extent of the requirements of all nine subject orders became apparent, teachers at KS2 were in agreement that it was impossible to teach all the National Curriculum. As one teacher put it: 'It's like eating the elephant bit by bit and you can only do what is possible' (Webb 1993a: 52). A consequence of chronic curriculum overload was that teachers viewed depth and quality as being sacrificed to achieve coverage and the basics, especially reading, as becoming neglected. Campbell (1994: 92) has argued that this particular difficulty was inevitable because the notional time allocations for English and mathematics given to the working groups were 'dramatically lower than was conventionally provided by primary teachers, according to every study that had examined time allocations in the post-war period'. Typically, in primary schools the basics occupied 50 per cent of the curriculum time available. English took up 30 per cent of time and mathematics 20 per cent, excluding their cross-curricular application. Furthermore, being 'document driven' as a result of the excessive prescription of the orders, meant that many teachers no longer felt able to respond spontaneously to children's interests or to unanticipated opportunities for learning.

In addition to the scope of the changes, the pace of National Curriculum change also inflicted enormous additional pressures upon teachers which at national level were all too readily dismissed as 'teething troubles'. As described by Dainton (1994: 7), 'the atmosphere in which the National Curriculum was introduced into schools was heavy-handed and punitive, with finger wagging civil servants insisting that "no one liked change but things would settle down"'. Many teachers who were conscientiously trying to do detailed lesson plans, acquire new knowledge in National Curriculum subjects, prepare materials for their lessons, mark work and maintain records of attainment, found it totally impossible to do everything properly and often felt exhausted, deskilled and demoralized (Webb 1993a).

In January 1993, during our first phase of fieldwork (September 1992–March 1993), the NCC issued its advice to the Secretary of State on the steps considered necessary to achieve the objectives of the ERA. This advice acknowledged that 'the National Curriculum is proving too complex and overprescriptive in practice' (NCC 1993a: 1) and recommended a rolling programme of review leading to the reduction of content in each subject order. David Pascall, the Chairman of the NCC until 19 April 1993, stressed the urgency of the need to address the problem of curriculum overload, which he recognized was particularly acute for primary schools, and pressed for the process of slimming down the National Curriculum to begin with the current revisions to the English and technology orders. These revised orders were scheduled for implementation in autumn 1994. His enthusiasm for revising the orders was at odds with the views of Richard Daugherty, Chairman of the Curriculum Council for Wales. While acknowledging the validity of the criticisms of the current orders and the manageability problems created for primary schools, Daugherty argued for a 'phase 2 of implementation within a largely stable framework of Orders and Regulations' in order to have 'time to develop a view of a new, modified framework' before rewriting the orders in 'phase 3' (Daugherty 1992: 14).

Despite unanimous agreement that the National Curriculum was overloaded and needed reducing in content, during the first phase of our fieldwork most teachers' views reflected those of Daugherty (1992). They wanted the National Curriculum to be left unchanged in order to provide a period of stability in which they could both reap the benefits of, and evaluate, the work that they had done. Also, teachers feared that revision of the orders might simply mean a restructuring of, rather than a reduction in, the content as they perceived to have been the case with the rewriting of the order for science published in 1991.

The demands of assessment

As the findings of Pollard *et al.*'s (1994) research demonstrate, the arrangements for national assessment marked a new and exceedingly contentious departure from established practice:

> In requiring teachers to implement externally derived tests, and in imposing on them externally determined requirements for recording and reporting children's progress and achievement, standardised national assessment represented what was arguably the most novel, the most coercive and the most difficult part of the 1988 Act's provisions to implement.
>
> (p. 207)

Between September 1987 and March 1988 a Task Group on Assessment and Testing (TGAT) devised a system of national assessment combining Standard Assessment Tasks (SATs) and Teacher Assessment (TA) to chart pupils' progress on a 10-level scale. The system was to serve formative, diagnostic, summative and evaluative purposes. Formative purposes were viewed as a priority because:

> We are required to propose a national assessment system which enhances teaching and learning without any increase in 'the calls on teachers' and pupils' time for activities which do not directly promote learning'.
>
> (TGAT 1988, para 24)

However, research into National Curriculum assessment led Gipps (1995) to stress: 'We understand now, beyond any doubt, that we cannot use one assessment across a range of purposes, although an assessment programme with a range of assessments in it may cover more than one purpose' (p. 8). Although TGAT did not associate TA with the formative function and tests with summative assessment, as national assessment was implemented these distinctions became more and more overt, becoming quite explicit in the later Dearing reports (1993a, 1993b).

Research on National Curriculum assessment at KS1 provides a critique of the SATs (NUT 1992), documents the enormous amount of time and effort invested by teachers in trying to make national assessment work (Campbell 1994) and reveals the stress, work overload and problems of classroom management and integration of tests with teaching experienced by teachers (NUT 1992; Pollard *et al.* 1994). However, through SATs acting as a training device, teachers' increasing experience of TA and the sharing of expertise through group moderation, gains have been made. Assessment in primary schools has moved from a largely intuitive approach to one based on evidence and written records which has enabled teachers to develop an improved understanding of what individual children can actually do – often accompanied by raised expectations – and to improve the rigour of their planning (Conner 1994; Gipps *et al*. 1994). Also, the process of moderation has 'forced teachers to interact, negotiate meanings of SoAs and hence standardise judgements made about individual children and "levelness"' (Gipps 1995: 11). However, as identified by James (1993), although teachers are becoming increasingly familiar with the processes involved in assessing and moderating, they experience difficulties in challenging the judgements of colleagues, since this runs contrary to the primary school culture which aims to be supportive rather than challenging, especially in the current climate which makes primary teachers feel particularly vulnerable.

The first statutory National Curriculum assessment at KS2 is scheduled for 1995, although a voluntary national pilot in the core subjects was initiated in 1994. The tests largely took the form of pencil and paper tests to be administered for a specified time to the whole class. The tests were marked by teachers according to 'mark schemes' because there was no provision for external marking or arrangements made for moderation. In contrast to national assessment at KS1, these tests, while infinitely more manageable, made little or no contribution to KS2 teachers' knowledge about assessment.

During the final stage of writing up the project's first report, members of the teachers' unions were balloted to gauge their support for a boycott of all forms of National Curriculum assessment and testing on the grounds that they were causing teachers to have excessive and unacceptable workloads – a claim that the findings of our report supported wholeheartedly (Webb 1993a). The proposal for a boycott, which rapidly expanded in scale and scope, originated in the English teachers' united opposition to the inadequately trialed KS3 English SATs which they believed both failed to represent the curriculum that they had been teaching and would lead to an impoverishment of children's linguistic and literary experience. In a speech to ATL on 7 April 1993 in which John Patten hoped to placate teachers and avoid such a boycott, he announced a review of the manageability of the National Curriculum and testing to be conducted by Sir Ron Dearing, Chairman of the new School Curriculum and Assessment Authority (SCAA) – also Chairman of NCC and School Examinations Assessment Council (SEAC) until the SCAA came into being in October 1993. However, instead of winning over the moderates, John Patten fuelled the mounting opposition from teachers, governors and parents by criticizing teachers for their 'unprofessional response' to concerns about testing and reaffirming the government's determination, despite all the objections, to ensure that the tests went ahead as planned (Patten 1993b). In a few months the three main teacher unions were engaged in industrial action to resist the 'unreasonable' workload generated by the National Curriculum assessment and testing. Although much of the testing at KS1 in 1993 had already taken place, participation in the boycott by primary teachers meant that the piloting of the KS2 SATs largely collapsed.

The future, post-Dearing

The Dearing review gave rise to two reports – an interim report (July 1993) and a final report (December 1993). The recommendations in the latter were accepted in full by the government and led to a review of all National Curriculum subjects and their assessment conducted by the SCAA. The final Dearing report (1993a) contains much discussion on the desirability or otherwise of moving from the 10-level scale to an alternative based on key stage programmes of study (PoS) and end of key stage grading scales indicating that the revision and simplification of national assessment was to be a vital part of the review. In order to carry out this review SCAA set up advisory groups (12–15 people) for each subject and key stage. The proposals for individual subjects were kept under scrutiny by the key stage advisory groups with a brief to ensure the curriculum as a whole was coherent and manageable. The whole process was overseen by a steering group of SCAA members and officers. The proposals for a slimmed down National Curriculum, although they drew extensively on the work of the advisory groups, were drafted by SCAA officers. This provoked some heated discussions, for example, in relation to the English proposals when the KS1 working group criticized Dearing's stress on Standard English for 7-year-olds against their advice. These proposals were accepted by the Secretary of State as the basis for consultation which ran from 9 May to 29 July and cost just under £2 million. The consultation revealed that the curriculum was still considered to be overloaded at KS2 and as a result further slimming down was undertaken (SCAA 1994). However, the proposals to move from statements of attainment to level descriptions were broadly welcomed. Level descriptions, which are mainly intended to inform pupils' end of key stage assessments, are the types and range of performance pupils characteristically demonstrate at each level.

   In the introduction to the report on the consultation Dearing claims that in revising the draft proposals:

> We have made some further reductions in content, but in response to demand, in a very small number of cases, we have reinserted some of the deletions. We have revised content to provide greater consistency of approach between subjects. We have refined the level descriptions. We have cut back on the verbiage. When we felt it

would help, we have provided exemplification within the documents; but let me underline, exemplification is for guidance: the decision is for the school.

(SCAA 1994: ii)

As demonstrated here, the process of National Curriculum revision was mainly a technical one of achieving manageability and structural consistency between subjects. The nature of the 10-subject National Curriculum and the aims, principles and priorities upon which it was based were neither up for debate in 1987, nor during the Dearing review. Tate (1994) gives a nod in that direction by asking the rhetorical question 'Have we got it right?' in relation to the balance between entitlement to a common culture and flexibility to cater for pupils' diverse needs in different ways. However, given the unprecedented effort and enormous expense already expended on the National Curriculum, a negative response was not likely to be entertained. Consequently, in the new orders sent into schools in January 1995, the basic subject framework remained largely intact, although information technology was removed from the technology order and is now a separate subject. The four key stages remain, although in reality the National Curriculum now ends at key stage 3 and to correspond with this the 10-level scale has been cut down to eight levels. At conferences set up to disseminate the results of the consultation (for example, Leeds, November 1994) emphasis was put on schools and teachers planning and implementing the National Curriculum, exercising freedom to meet the needs of their pupils through:

- the teaching methods adopted;
- the choice provided by leaving 20 per cent of time free from the National Curriculum;
- the notion of teaching aspects of the PoS in depth or in outline.

If teachers are encouraged to work freely with the latter notion, then apart from Year 2 and Year 6 which are directly affected by the tests, schools may feel able to make curriculum decisions on the basis of educational rather than logistical reasons and to decide which curriculum areas to emphasize or new areas to introduce.

The new National Curriculum is due to begin in September 1995. However, serious doubts remain about whether it will be possible to teach it plus religious education (RE) within 80 per cent of the recommended minimum weekly teaching time at KS1 and 2. As demonstrated by Alexander and Campbell (1994), the curricular arithmetic by which schools are allocated 20 per cent of curriculum time for discretionary use does not stand up to scrutiny. Campbell (1994) explains that the times allocated to English and mathematics are dramatically lower than current practice; there is no evidence to justify Dearing's assertion that KS2 children need less time for English than those at KS1; time for science is less than that previously suggested to the science working group as necessary; national testing will reinforce undue emphasis on the core subjects; inadequate time is allocated to the other foundation subjects; and too much time has been set aside for RE. Campbell (1994: 98) concludes:

> Thus Dearing's solution to the curriculum manageability problem was to draw on a mechanistic arithmetic which enabled him to pretend to a retained commitment to the broad and balanced curriculum, while leaving in place all the old pressures in the primary school culture to concentrate on the basics at the expense of other subjects.

The government's solution to the workload issue is to commit over £30 million to the appointment of external markers at KS2 and KS3 and to provide additional supply cover at KS1 in an attempt to ensure that the tests go ahead in 1995. TA is to have, as Dearing recommended, 'equal standing' in reporting to parents. However, as James (1994: 13) argues, only the summative scores will be 'visible' and the high profile statutory testing programme 'will inevitably be the measure of teacher assessment because of the importance and resources attached to it'. SCAA will be developing advice on the quality assurance of TA which is likely to include exemplification materials to help teachers match level descriptions to pupils' performance. However, the mandatory audit of TA at KS1 has ended and the new Grants for Education, Support and Training (GEST) arrangements provide no further support for assessment training and moderation between schools. There is now a massive concentration of effort and funding on the testing element of national assessment. This is to the detriment of TA which has the potential to make a substantial and lasting contribution to teacher professional development and the quality of learning. At KS2 the reporting of test results will give the tests added emphasis. However, only time will tell just how far what is taught and how it is taught, especially in Year 6, will change to match the demands and system of testing.

Classroom practice under scrutiny

While the National Curriculum prescribes what should be taught, how it should be taught remains the preserve of teachers. For example, the DES (1989a) states 'it is important to note that':

> the way in which teaching is timetabled and how lessons are described and organised cannot be prescribed;
> The organisation of the curriculum to deliver national requirements

and support LEAs' and governors' curricular policies is a matter for
the headteacher.

(para 4.3)

This principle has constantly been reiterated but in a context where
increasingly the approaches to classroom organization and teaching
methods in primary education have been the subject of political and
media attention. Following the publication of the findings of the
evaluation of the Leeds LEA Primary Needs Project (PNP) (Alexander
1992), this attention intensified. Unfortunately, it has been characterized
by what Ball (1990c) calls 'the discourse of derision' with simplistic
caricatured notions of 'informal' 'progressive' education being the subject
of attack. Kenneth Clarke, the then Secretary of State, who had made his
dislike of progressive child-centred education well known (see for
example, Clarke 1991) in December 1991 called upon Professor Robin
Alexander, Jim Rose, Chief Inspector for HMI and Chris Woodhead,
Chief Executive of the NCC ' "to review available evidence about the
delivery of education in primary schools" and "to make recommendations about curriculum organization, teaching methods and classroom practice appropriate for the successful implementation of the
National Curriculum, particularly at Key Stage 2" ' (Alexander *et al.*
1992: 5). Woods and Wenham (1994) provide a fascinating analysis
of the career of the subsequent document – the DES Discussion
Paper *Curriculum Organisation and Classroom Practice in Primary Schools*
(Alexander *et al.* 1992) – and explore the reasons why it was received with
both hostile opposition and strong support according to whether it was
accepted as a paper 'to initiate a discussion, not to impose solutions'
(Alexander *et al.* 1992: 5), regarded as a definitive report, an academic
paper or a political document. They suggest its career can be conceived of
in two broad stages,

> the political, when the policies of the 'New Right' dictated the
> course and reception of the action; and the educational, when the
> document was mediated into practice through the LEA ('showing
> strategic leadership') and the headteachers (acting as 'gatekeepers')
> and appropriated by classroom teachers.
>
> (Alexander *et al.* 1992: 1)

Although described as providing 'a basis for the debate which the
Secretary of State wishes to promote' (Alexander *et al.* 1992: 5), at
national level in the document's 'political' stage there was no debate:

> In effect, the debate was opened, judged and closed in the same
> document. Progressive child-centred methods and the Plowden
> report were subjected to a public deconstruction, progressive

teachers were disciplined and the groundwork was laid for a thoroughgoing reintroduction of traditional teaching methods.

(Ball 1994: 44)

As the first phase of our fieldwork revealed (Webb 1993a), in its 'educational' stage, some LEAs sought to use the paper to stimulate a review of classroom practice through courses, conferences, and working parties set up to produce and publish an LEA response (for example, Lancashire County Council 1992). The extent to which the document was the subject of discussion or INSET at school level was very variable and, as Woods and Wenham (1994) found, it depended on the head-teachers' views of the document and how they might use it to their advantage. As regards individual teachers, after interviewing six teachers in mid-career about the document, Woods and Wenham (1994: 43) concluded that:

> reactions varied depending on the teachers' own personal values and on school ethos. Anything that was unacceptable could be resisted by non-compliance. They viewed the paper on the whole as endowing retrospective validation of practices in their classrooms rather than initiating new ones . . . where they disagreed with the paper they sharpened their own beliefs through contrastive definition without fear of being legislated against.

Unsurprisingly, a year later, the OFSTED (1993a: 18) follow-up report found that: 'the culture of primary teaching has not changed overnight. It would be unrealistic to expect a discussion paper to bring about changes in this or that aspect of practice'. In a letter to primary schools accompanying the OFSTED (1993a) and NCC (1993a) reports, Patten asked teachers to address, among other issues, the introduction of setting and ability grouping, greater use of subject teaching and teaching by subject specialists, further improvement in the planning of topic work, more use of whole class teaching, limiting the number of activities taking place in classrooms at one time and the development of the role of the head as curriculum leader. Since then, these recommendations have been re-emphasized and further developed (for example, OFSTED 1994b) and have become the official stance on what constitutes best practice.

In his first annual lecture as Her Majesty's Chief Inspector for Schools, Chris Woodhead criticized child-centred education, echoing the DES Discussion Paper's (Alexander *et al*. 1992) references to teachers unthinkingly subscribing to 'Plowdenism' (Alexander *et al*. 1992: 10). He argued that the immediate need was to turn from preoccupation with recent legislation in order to make a priority: 'our vision of the educational good, our expectations of what children can and should achieve and the teaching methods we use as we seek to initiate our pupils into the best that has been thought and said' (Hackett 1995: 3). Few primary teachers would argue with his assertion that the focus should return to teaching and learning, especially the latter. However, the ways in which he might use his position to direct this focus and also his lack of acknowledgement of the context in which primary teachers are working – which for many is one of diminishing resources, teacher redundancy and increases in class size – are extremely worrying.

The average class size in KS2 in our sample schools in autumn 1992 – spring 1993 was 26 pupils. The more generous staffing structures to be found in small schools meant that the average class in small schools was 22, whereas it was 27 in the medium size schools and 29 in the large schools. Throughout the research period there was concern in the schools that class sizes were rising, which is borne out by Bennett's (1994) national survey of class size which found that almost one in three teachers was teaching a class of over 30 children and that the situation was worst in KS2 where nearly 40 per cent taught such classes. To try to keep class sizes down, teachers without class responsibilities were being given classes, thus reducing staffing flexibility, and pupils were being shared equitably among teachers, thereby often creating mixed age classes. Politicians, unwilling to accept that class size has adverse effects on pupils' learning, point to a lack of conclusive evidence on this issue, but without acknowledging that this lack is because the appropriate British research has yet to be carried out. However, experimental research in North America – project STAR (Student Teacher Achievement Ratio) in the state of Tennessee, which compared pupil achievement in three types of classes: small classes (13–17), regular classes (22–25) and regular size classes supported by a full-time teacher aide within 79 schools – has concluded that small classes resulted in improved pupil progress in the short term and up to two years up to re-entry into regular classes (Nye *et al.* 1992; Achilles *et al.* 1993). Countries such as Korea, which has an average primary class size of 55 and yet in which pupils produce work of a high standard (Burstall 1992), are also cited as evidence that rises in class size need not be harmful and, if accompanied by whole class teaching and streaming, might even improve the quality of teaching. However, the potential impact of class size obviously has to be considered in conjunction with the cultural context, curriculum demands, available resources and the range of ages, abilities, motivation and special educational needs within each class. The rationale for smaller classes given by teachers in our research was to ensure sufficient attention was given to individuals; to enable pupils to engage in the discussions, investigations and problem solving required by the National Curriculum; to avoid overcrowding in classrooms often built for smaller numbers; to reduce teachers' workloads – especially in relation to assessment and record keeping; and to make schools more marketable as parents were perceived to prefer schools with small classes.

In this context of mounting pressures on schools to change, it is more necessary than ever that whole schools and the individual teachers of which they are comprised should be very clear about, and able to articulate, the beliefs, experiences and purposes underpinning their approaches to teaching, not only to justify them but also to develop and maintain control over them. The next chapter, which presents our findings on classroom practice at KS2, provides an overview of classroom organization and pedagogical issues, giving the views of teachers in the research schools and drawing on their wealth of experience to offer advice.

Moving towards a partnership with governors

The evolution of governing bodies in England and Wales is charted by Maclure (1988) who examines in detail their powers and duties under the ERA. An important contribution to that evolution was the work of the Taylor Committee which was set up by the Labour Government and published its report in 1977 (DES/Welsh Office 1977). The report recommended a strengthening of the powers of governors and major changes in the composition of governing bodies, with membership shared equally between LEA representatives, teachers, the parents and the local community. The Education Act 1986, the major piece of legislation as far as governing bodies is concerned, revised the composition of the governing bodies in line with the Taylor Report (DES/Welsh Office 1977) and extended their powers over the curriculum and the conduct of the school. These powers were consolidated and further enhanced by the passing of the ERA which devolved to them many of the duties previously performed by LEAs. As has been documented (Dodds 1994) and will be addressed in Chapter 6, the development of an effective partnership between schools and their governing bodies has not been without its problems for schools and governors alike. However, while at school level there are many difficulties still to be overcome, governing bodies have established themselves as a vital group within the educational establishment, as is demonstrated by the formation of the National Governors Council (NGC) launched in autumn 1994. The NGC, which is rapidly establishing links with the estimated 350,000 governors in England and Wales, is emerging as a potentially powerful pressure group in the campaign against the underfunding of schools.

Implications of local management of schools

The introduction of LMS, involving both the delegation by LEAs to schools and governors of financial responsibility and matters relating to staffing, represented a major change in the work of headteachers and the ways in which schools are run. Originally only primary schools with over 200 pupils were involved, but in September 1991 LMS was extended to primary schools of all sizes. The budget payable to an individual school and placed under the management of the governing body was to be determined by formula funding crucially involving age-weighted pupil units. The rationale for LMS was that this would lead to greater commitment, efficiency and value for money on the part of governors and their schools once local bureaucracy was stripped away. Successful pilot schemes in Solihull and Cambridgeshire demonstrated how budgetary control could be devolved to governors and school staffs and the potential benefits to the schools. For the first time the possibility was opened up for schools to view the curriculum, school organization, resources and the budget as an interrelated whole and to appreciate the implications of decisions in one area for the development of another.

From the outset, there was concern that a market economy would lock schools with catchments in deprived areas and few opportunities to generate income into a descending spiral of underfunding and low achievement, thus exacerbating social inequities in educational provision (Ball 1990a; Brown 1990). Also, the growing demands made on school spending – for example, in resourcing the National Curriculum, information technology (IT) provision and computerized school administration and salary rises – means schools are likely to need additional funding simply to maintain and update provision. However, if government funding is not forthcoming and local authorities' expenditure continues to be capped, it is unclear where the funding will come from or whether schools will suffer from decreasing funds in real terms.

Owing to the delegation of budgets to schools under LMS, schools opting out of LEA control into grant maintained status and the new arrangements for registered inspections, the in-service training and support provided by LEAs has diminished. A survey of 62 LEAs (Dean 1994) reported that nine mentioned INSET as a particularly threatened area of their work and that across the LEAs 'respondents referred to discontinued support in all aspects of the curriculum, in primary education, appraisal, home/school relationships, audio-visual service, management training and newly-qualified teachers' (p. 7). Our first research report (Webb 1993a, Chapter 6) examined the advice on National Curriculum implementation at KS2 provided by LEAs. The 13 LEAs in our study were variously engaged in the provision of courses and guidance on planning at KS2, but they were doing this in a context of reduced funding, time and staffing to be spent on such work. They were at different stages in the process of moving from the traditional centralized model of INSET organization towards an agency-based model prepared to compete with other INSET suppliers in the free market which involved the redeployment and reduction of staff, especially advisory teachers. The main strategy being developed for the provision of primary INSET was to offer service agreements operating at various levels into which schools could buy. The second round of fieldwork (November 1993–February 1994) found schools reviewing these agreements and considering whether to opt for a lower level of service than they had purchased previously in order to retain more funds and to increase flexibility.

A major consequence of the restructuring of INSET provision was that teachers at KS2 generally did not receive the same depth of support and coordinated INSET provision on planning, implementing and assessing the National Curriculum as their colleagues at KS1. While initially schools found it difficult to conceptualize the implications of these changes, the second period of fieldwork revealed how rapidly they had adjusted to their altered circumstances and were becoming more confident in providing their own INSET and increasingly cooperating with other schools and drawing on the expertise of a range of INSET providers. Chapter 4 discusses how the provision of INSET for colleagues has become a new and demanding role for coordinators.

Competition in the market place

The parents' charter which was published in 1991 and updated in 1994 claims that 'under the Government's reforms you should get all the information you need to keep track of your child's progress, to find out how the school is being run, and to compare all local schools' (DFE 1994: 3). The key documents to provide this information are:

- a written report on a child's progress written at least once a year;
- regular reports from OFSTED inspectors;
- performance tables;
- school brochures;
- an annual report from the school's governors.

Thus as Maclure (1988: 24–5) argues:

Parents are intended under the Act to become more discriminating consumers, watching school results, as published, and interpreting these results as best they can in the light of local circumstances. The assumption is that they will keep schools up to the mark by making their approval or disapproval known in informal contacts with governors and teachers, and through their formal opportunity to raise points (and pass resolutions) at the annual parents meeting required by the 1986 Act.

In order significantly to increase parental choice of school for their children, under the ERA schools were also required to enrol pupils up to their agreed physical capacity, with as few exceptions as possible. It was the government's intention that in a competitive market popular schools would command parental support and expand and therefore the producers of education, the schools, would have to comply with the wishes of the parents as consumers. Thus open enrolment has created the conditions for competition between schools and encouraged them to improve their public image and actively market themselves through devices such as school brochures, features in local newpapers, TV and radio programmes and events for parents. Advice on how best to go about this new dimension of a headteacher's role is appearing in manuals for headteachers (Harrison and Gill 1992; Dean 1995) and books specifically on marketing (Hardie 1991). Chapter 6 reveals the effects on the role of headteachers of the move to parents as consumers.

Management for quality

Since the introduction of the ERA, there have been mounting pressures from the government for schools to improve standards and the quality of the education that they provide. The most potent force for quality assurance are the inspections of the Office for Standards in Education (OFSTED), which was established by the 1992 Education Act. The nature of the inspection process is described in the *Handbook for the Inspection of Schools* (OFSTED 1993b). As explained by Clegg and Billington (1994: 2), in their advice to primary schools on how to make the most of their inspection, unlike the LEA inspections:

> The purpose is not to support and advise, it is to collect a range of evidence, match the evidence against a statutory set of criteria, arrive at judgements and make those judgements known to the public. Put bluntly, OFSTED inspections are not designed to help individual schools do a better job, they are designed to come to a judgement about the quality of the job which they are currently doing. Once the judgements are made and the report is written, it is the responsibility of the school, and in particular the governors, to come up with a plan to indicate how they will make any improvements deemed necessary by the inspection.

The inspections of secondary schools started in September 1993 and for primary schools in September 1994. However, from the outset OFSTED was unable to meet its first term timetable of 1,290 primary inspections in order to meet the government pledge enshrined in the 1992 Act to inspect all 18,000 English primaries within a four-year cycle. This shortfall arose owing to a combination of a national shortage of primary inspectors, the complexity and perceived fickleness of the process of tendering for inspection contracts and the intensity of the inspection process which meant inspection teams were reluctant or unable to try to meet OFSTED'S goal of seven or eight inspections a week (Sweetman 1994). Currently, to take account of inspection experience and changes to the National Curriculum OFSTED is drawing up guidance for inspectors to use until the framework is revised in September 1996. This guidance is expected to acknowledge that the existing framework is based on a secondary model and to suggest a temporary primary-focused alternative which recognizes the realities of primary schools and in particular that the predominance of topic work and block timetabling of aspects of subjects means that not every subject may be taught during the course of an inspection.

Another potentially important mechanism for monitoring and improving quality in teaching and learning is teacher appraisal. Following pilot schemes, the report of the National Steering Group on appraisal was published in 1989. However, the formal implementation of appraisal was deferred to allow National Curriculum implementation to be a priority and probably also to delay the costs involved. Eventually in the face of criticism over the delay, the government made regulations under the 1986 Education Act (DES 1991a) which came into force in August 1991 making it a duty for LEAs (where appropriate) and governing bodies in grant maintained schools to ensure that every teacher was formally appraised between 1992 and 1994. However, no national form of appraisal was implemented and LEAs and schools were required to work out their own training and procedures. Our data revealed this to be a very low priority for teachers. Appraisal appears to have been overshadowed by the multiple demands of the ERA and the inspection process. As reported by the Leverhulme Teacher Appraisal Project (Wragg *et al.* 1994: 21), for the appraisal process 'to be meaningful it needs to be carried out properly and be conducted with due care and consideration' and 'finding the time to do this is regarded as being the biggest obstacle'.

The School Development Plan and the thought and discussion giving rise to it can provide a major forum for bringing together budgetary decisions and plans for developments in the curriculum, teachers' professional development and pupil learning. The process of target setting tied to review also serves as a quality assurance mechanism. Holly and Southworth (1989) suggest that the idea of school development plans was first actively promoted in the ILEA's Report of the Committee on Primary Education (ILEA 1985). Their recommendations were then taken up by the House of Commons Select Committee in their report (1986). To try to promote a more nationally coherent approach in 1989 the DES funded the School Development Plan project to identify good practice and develop advice for LEAs, schools and governing bodies (Hargreaves and Hopkins 1991). Now almost all schools have a development plan of some kind but, as discussed in Chapter 7, they vary enormously in purpose, clarity of goals, detail, those who have contributed to them and the part they play in the management process.

This chapter has briefly examined those legislative changes and associated government initiatives which gave rise to the situation of multiple innovations that the primary schools portrayed within subsequent chapters sought to cope with and to control. The changing roles and responsibilities of classteachers, coordinators, deputy headteachers and headteachers were a necessary response to the number and scope of these innovations and the speed with which they were introduced. It is to these changing roles and responsibilities that we now turn.

two

Changing demands on classroom practice

The DES discussion paper (Alexander *et al.* 1992), the origins of which were briefly discussed in Chapter 1, recommends that teachers should select the most appropriate organizational strategy – whole class teaching, group work or individual teaching – to fit the purpose of the lesson. They note that, at KS1, teachers spend about a third of their time on whole class teaching which was confirmed by the researchers in the Leverhulme Primary Project (Wragg 1993) from their observations of 60 primary teachers. However, as Alexander *et al.* (1992) point out, because traditions of individual and group work are stronger at KS1, the proportion of whole class teaching may be higher at KS2. Since the claim in the discussion paper that 'in many schools the benefits of whole class teaching have been insufficiently exploited' (p. 35), there has been increasing pressure on teachers from OFSTED and the government both to improve the quality of their whole class teaching and to use this strategy more frequently. Consequently, we were interested to discover through our research the ways in which the National Curriculum was taught at KS2 and the prevalence of whole class teaching. The first section in this chapter presents the findings of our classroom observations and discusses the usefulness of the notion of 'fitness for purpose' in the planning and evaluating of approaches to teaching in the light of those findings.

This is followed by consideration of the clear message coming through classroom research over the last 20 years that the crucial factor in improving pupils' learning, whatever approaches are employed, is that all children should experience, as often as possible, sustained higher-order work-related interactions with the teacher. Cooperative groupwork provides the opportunity for increasing pupil work-related talk and yet it

Table 2.1　Per cent of lessons with different class and curriculum organizational strategies (N = 54)

1 Whole class teaching (teacher–pupil interaction throughout)	18.5
2 Whole class teaching (input plus tasks)	31.5
3 Two groups	5.6
4 Carousel within subject/topic	9.3
5 Carousel across subjects and topic	14.8
6 Cooperative group work	7.4
7 Menu	9.3
8 Individual work	3.7

appears to be a very underused approach. The reasons for this are explored and advice offered on how to introduce or improve the quality of cooperative group work. While pupils may seldom work in groups, they frequently sit in them. Alternative seating arrangements are reviewed, followed by a consideration of ability grouping and other means of achieving differentiation in order to create more favourable conditions for learning. As discussed in Chapter 1, an enormous amount of thought and work has gone into TA since the introduction of National Curriculum assessment. The chapter concludes with some examples of the ways in which teachers are building assessment into the tasks and activities given to pupils and the contributions pupils can make to their own self-evaluation.

Classroom and curriculum organizational strategies

In our research, fieldnotes were made of the 54 lessons observed in order to provide detailed descriptions of the range of experiences offered to pupils in KS2 and to look for common patterns. We found the observations could be categorized into eight lesson patterns based on organizational strategies combined with approaches to curriculum organization (see Table 2.1). The lessons observed generally occurred between morning break and lunchtime or lunchtime and afternoon break and included all areas of the curriculum with the exception of music and PE.

There were two categories of whole class teaching which, as is explained below, differed mainly in that the second incorporated some individual work by pupils. It is interesting to note that these lessons comprise 50 per cent of the total of observed lessons – a higher proportion of whole class teaching than that reported by OFSTED (1993a) in the

HMI survey of 74 schools in the summer term of 1992. While this might simply be a reflection of different samples, it also raises the question as to whether HMI samples might at that time have been systematically biased towards group and individual teaching. This could occur because, first, past HMI reports had bemoaned the lack of good group work in primary schools and, second, teachers may be less inclined to whole class teach when being observed by an inspector because it is more stressful, since they become the focus of attention and their interactions with pupils are more readily evaluated. While recognizing, therefore, the limitations of our own classroom data as reliable and valid quantitative measures, they do at least raise the issue as to whether the government's perceptions of the need for more whole class teaching (see Patten 1993a) are not based on questionable assumptions as to the extent of whole class teaching now taking place.

In the first of our categories of whole class teaching, the teacher interacted with the whole class for the majority of the lesson – half an hour or more – explaining the subject matter of the lesson, seeking comments from pupils and asking questions. An example is the whole class lesson on the Chinese New Year given by a junior school teacher which is described in Box 2.1.

Box 2.1   Example of whole class teaching (category 1)
The teacher began by telling the children in her Year 3 class the legend associated with the Chinese New Year and asking them questions about it. Then she explained the Chinese 12-year cycle whereby each year has an animal associated with it and the children worked out the animal symbol for the year in which they were born. She showed them some New Year cards and invited comments about the design and the message inside written in Chinese characters. Next she gave out red 'lucky bags' and the children opened them, sampled the Chinese sweets and compared the pictures and writing on the bags. The teacher went on to describe the shop where she had bought the New Year items and the menu in the Chinese restaurant next door. This led into a discussion about the kinds of Chinese food the children had eaten and how this was cooked. Then the children got out the atlases to locate China and to suggest alternative ways of getting there. Finally, they all copied the characters making up the message 'Best Wishes for a Happy New Year' into their exercise books. While they were doing this the teacher went around the class asking recall questions about the knowledge on China that she had covered. Finally, she went to the cupboard and took out two Chinese bamboo wall hangings, asked the children to describe them and told them that in a future lesson they would be making similar hangings. As a follow-up activity after lunch the children were required to complete a piece of cloze procedure on the legend and to draw one of the pictures on the 'lucky bags'.

Box 2.2   Example of whole class teaching (category 2)

As part of their topic on water the children in Year 3/4 had looked at some aspects of the local environment, especially along the nearby river bank. The teacher began by getting the children to brainstorm aspects of the landscape they thought should be considered and she wrote these on the blackboard. She then went through each aspect with the class and they decided whether it was appropriate, if it could be subsumed under one of the other suggestions and what would need to be included under such a heading. After 25 minutes of interacting with the whole class, the teacher wrote the title and date on the board and the children began writing using the ideas on the board as a framework. After 20 minutes of working quietly on the task, the teacher stopped the class and asked for four volunteers to read out their descriptions. The teacher commented on the strengths of the descriptions and how they might be improved further and offered general reminders to the class such as 'Don't forget your capital letters for place names please'. The descriptions were to be finished after lunch.

This lesson, which lasted approximately an hour, enabled the teacher to introduce a considerable amount of information. Through a variety of recall and open-ended questions she drew on the children's prior experience and maintained their attention through the resources she used, changes of activity and a lively presentational style while moving around the classroom. Throughout the lesson, most of the pupils most of the time appeared to be motivated and engaged in the work. They followed the teachers' instructions and were keen to answer questions. Only a very few reminders were needed to keep the children on task.

In the second category of whole class lessons teachers provided an introductory input of around 15 to 20 minutes before setting the pupils the same or similar related tasks. Throughout the rest of such lessons teachers periodically requested the attention of the whole class in order to provide further instructions, to comment on the work in progress, to ask children to present to their peers what they had done and to seek evaluative comments on their work. See for example the description in Box 2.2 where in a Year 3/4 class in a primary school the teacher wanted the children to identify and record key characteristics of the local landscape around the school in order that when they went on a forthcoming visit to a different geographical area they could draw comparisons.

A notable feature of both these whole class lessons was the control the teacher exerted over the pace and direction of the lesson. In the second example, children reading their work aloud appeared to act as a model of both the kinds of content required and what might reasonably be achieved within the timescale.

Box 2.3 Example of teaching using two groups (category 3)
The teacher, who had 23 Year 3/4 pupils in a small square classroom, sat them in groups of four to six children with the oldest on one side of the room and the youngest on the other. In the lesson observed the teacher worked with each group in turn by sitting with them and explaining the tasks set and questioning them to test their understanding. She worked on sentence construction and the use of capital letters and full stops with the younger group while the older ones did mathematics from textbooks. Then, while the Year 3s completed a worksheet practising the grammar that she had taught them, she sat with the older ones and went through the answers to some mental arithmetic that they had done. The children who were working on their own did so quietly and did not interrupt her teaching of the others.

Category 3, which was derived from three mixed age classes, was where the teacher taught each age range in turn. The nature of the teacher–pupil interactions was very similar to that observed in lessons in Categories 1 and 2 except that the smaller size of group allowed for more sustained discussion with individual children. See, for example, in Box 2.3 the description of how mathematics and English were taught to a Year 3/4 class in a primary school.

The fact that the teacher could teach each group in turn undisturbed was clearly vital to the success of this approach. She explained that she had accustomed her class to this way of working which involved encouraging them to be independent and to be willing to seek, and to give, assistance to their peers.

Group work, whereby tasks were rotated around the groups on a carousel system, was observed in 24.1 per cent of lessons. The tasks required children to work individually and/or in pairs. Depending on the complexity of the tasks, children either worked on one task for the entire lesson or the tasks were rotated around the groups once or twice during the lesson. While the classroom organization and teaching techniques were very similar in all the carousel group work observed, Category 4 and Category 5 reflect alternative forms of curriculum organization. In Category 4 all the tasks were within one subject or subject-focused topic – for example, a science lesson on earth in space for Year 4 pupils taught by a science specialist. In this lesson the children were organized into four groups working on the following activities: cloze procedure about the phases of the moon followed by sequencing drawings of the phases; making information booklets on the moon using 'cue cards' of questions to guide their research in reference books; making a model to show the tilt of the earth and its relationship to the seasons; completing a worksheet on the hours of daylight throughout the seasons and recording this information on a graph. In examples such as this, where all the group tasks focused on a particular subject or topic, carousel group work was one of a range of approaches used both within that subject/topic and in other subjects. Thus the science specialist explained that she also used whole class teaching, cooperative group work and individual work depending mainly on the potential for investigative work of the aspect of science to be taught and the resources available to support such work. This example challenges the stereotype of subject teaching as involving didactic teaching to the whole class, which is sometimes forwarded as an argument against its suitability for primary children.

In Category 5, where the group tasks represented different subjects, of which topic might be the focus of one or two of the tasks, carousel group work was the predominant – though not usually the only – approach used in that class. For example, in a small primary school a Year 3/4 class was working in four groups on the following activities: painting dragons as a follow-up activity to a story about Beowulf; completing a geography worksheet based on the previous day's input which required finding places in atlases and maps; working in pairs to write poems about dragons (this involved writing descriptive sentences, cutting sentences out and rearranging them into the most logical and interesting order); and working with the teacher to produce a group poem. It is interesting that most carousels only involved four group activities. This suggests that teachers in KS2 tend to have fewer groups operating simultaneously than in KS1. Alternatively, notice may have been taken of the PNP evaluation (Alexander 1992) which stressed the problems that can occur when the teacher has too many groups to manage and the subsequent advice on reducing the number of such group activities made in the DES discussion paper (Alexander *et al.* 1992: 29).

Only four lessons (7.4 per cent) involved children working in cooperative groups – that is groups where children were intended to work together on a shared outcome. For example, a Year 4 class in a primary school was working in small groups on the same experiment which involved rolling a cotton reel down a card slope into various barriers and, first, predicting what they thought would happen and, second, recording what actually happened. Each barrier was to be 'tested' several times. The main aim of the lesson was to introduce children to making predictions and the secondary purpose was to help them to appreciate the need to standardize variables in order to carry out a fair test. One lesson was observed where the cooperative groups were also 'expert' groups. In a topic lesson in a Year 6 class in a middle school, the children were put in an imaginary situation where a motor racing circuit was to be constructed in the grounds of a rural stately home that they had visited. They were asked to join one of three groups which represented the circuit

---

Box 2.4   Using a menu system (category 7)

In a Year 4 class the classroom was divided up into five bases: mathematics, language, science, art/design and 'a spare table for whatever we need to do that week' – often history or geography. The week's activities for each area were planned cooperatively by the three Year 4 teachers and the Section 11 teacher to ensure continuity of experience between classes. Children were able to select the order in which they worked through the activities with the one rule that 'if the table is full you can't choose that activity'. The activities were planned to enable children to work on them independently and in order to release the teacher to work in depth with individuals and groups. The children were each assigned to one of five ability groups, named after famous people, and throughout the day the teacher called these groups together in order to go over the work set and to teach new content and skills – predominantly in the core subjects. As all except two children in the class were Asian, the teacher considered an emphasis on literacy to be very important. While some of the menu activities in the bases were the same for all children, others were differentiated according to the ability groups and labelled accordingly so that the children knew which activity they should do. In order to monitor pupil progress through the National Curriculum teachers needed detailed records of both menu and non-menu work. Therefore, each classteacher was given about an hour a week of non-contact time to assist with record keeping. Also, pupils were encouraged to record the work that they had done in each subject. While this form of classroom organization was highly complex, it was felt to be advantageous in creating time for the sustained interaction with individuals that was thought to be particularly necessary when children were second language learners. Problems, such as those created by children who found it difficult to work independently or who without intervention from the teacher would experience an imbalance of work over the day, were identified and discussed by the whole staff. Towards the end of 1992 the school's menu policy had been revised to incorporate advice on these and other issues.

---

designers, environmentalists who were opposed to the scheme and owners of the stately home who needed to diversify to generate more income. In the lesson observed the groups were marshalling their arguments prior to presenting them to each other and to a Year 7 class who were to be called upon to adjudicate.

In five (9.3 per cent) of the lessons observed children were working according to a menu system. See for example Box 2.4 for the description of a lesson in an inner city first school (311 pupils) where a menu system was the main organizational strategy adopted throughout the school.

One small school also operated a menu of tasks from which children selected their work within a carousel of four activities. This has been assigned to Category 7 because the choice offered the children in order to promote their independence and to share out resources including teacher time was its key feature. In the other cases where a menu system was operating, these involved tasks being written on the board. The children were required to do all of the tasks but they could opt to tackle them in any order. Some of the tasks were those resulting from whole class lessons, group and individual work on previous days, or earlier in the day, that needed completion. On a Friday several teachers said that they had one or two lessons organized in this way in order to ensure that pupils had as little unfinished work as possible to carry over to the next week.

For some part of many of the lessons in each category children worked on tasks individually. However, only two of the lessons observed consisted solely of children following individual programmes of work. Category 8 included a mathematics lesson and an English lesson where all pupils worked individually at their own pace and level from graded textbooks within a scheme. As will be demonstrated in the next section, lessons comprising a high proportion of individual work of whatever kind have been criticized for keeping the teacher extremely busy while pupils who encounter difficulties waste time queuing for assistance. One teacher who had a Year 6 class described how he mainly worked through individualized instruction, although when he started a new aspect of a topic or subject he would do a whole class input. Often the children were working on two or three subject areas and towards the end of the week in the 'tying up of loose ends' sessions there might be nine or 10 different activities occurring simultaneously. In order to cope with children needing help, especially in mathematics and English, he had introduced a system that he had devised with a colleague in a previous school which was similar to that used to control queuing in delicatessens. Children who needed help took a card with a number on it. When he called out a child's number the child put up his or her hand and the teacher went to give the required help. Any children overcoming their difficulties prior to their numbers being called kept their cards until he said their numbers. As he discovered when he first set up the system, if they did not do this then the cards got out of order and the system broke down.

The above examples serve as illustrations of the range of ways in which children are being taught the National Curriculum. Teachers are urged to apply the notion of 'fitness for purpose' both to make decisions about which teaching approach to adopt to meet their lesson objectives (Alexander *et al.* 1992) and to evaluate their lessons (OFSTED 1994b). Talking to teachers during the research made it clear that availability of resources was an important determinant in the selection of teaching approaches. It may be regarded as preferable to have all the children in a class in groups engaging simultaneously in the same science experiment, but insufficient equipment could mean that groups have to take it in turns to do the experiment while the rest of the class works on one or more other tasks. The constraints imposed by a large class of over 35 pupils in cramped conditions might lead a teacher to demonstrate an experiment rather than attempt to manage practical group work. Also, as argued by Stone (1993), based on her research into the introduction of the National Curriculum in a junior and infants school, when teachers taught in ways with which they were less familiar – even though they might perceive these methods as highly desirable – they experienced anxiety and dissatisfaction. Teachers' subject knowledge also influenced their choice of approaches as their range was more extensive when teaching to their subject strengths. If teachers are to enlarge their repertoires, more support for the development of subject knowledge and pedagogy needs to be provided both within school and through INSET.

The teachers in our study, whatever the extent of their teaching repertoires, had preferred styles based on their own particular skills, experiences and personalities. For example, the Year 3 teacher described in the first example of a whole class lesson considered that, whilst she used a range of methods, she was at her most effective when teaching the whole class. In some cases an increase in teaching repertoires may require a change in values or beliefs which, as Fullan (1991) suggests, may be difficult because these are often deeply rooted and not made explicit. As Nias (1989) has argued, the way in which teachers teach is an expression of their identity and self-image. Consequently, 'fitness for persons' seems to be equally as important as 'fitness for purpose'. Also, of fundamental importance in the notion of 'fitness for persons' must be ensuring that the teaching approach used is appropriate for the children. The whole class lessons described, which appeared very effective in their particular school contexts, would have been regarded as likely to be ineffective in the classroom situation depicted in Box 2.4, where some of the Asian pupils were in the early stages of learning English and would have been unable to follow a whole class lesson. These pupils were accustomed to receiving differentiated activities rather than trying to adjust to teaching aimed at the middle of the ability range of the class. In addition, as research into learning styles suggests, pupils have preferred learning styles in the same way that teachers have preferred teaching styles (Pike and Selby 1988). On occasion this might be able to be taken into account through various forms of differentiation, such as those discussed later in this chapter. However, it is also an argument for ensuring that children experience a range of teaching approaches in order to improve their opportunities for learning and to help them to recognize the ways in which they learn most readily.

The importance of teacher–pupil interaction

In the introduction to this chapter, emphasis was placed on the importance of teacher–pupil interactions in promoting pupil learning. Therefore it seems worth while briefly to recap the lessons on this issue to be derived from past research. The Observational Research and Classroom Learning Evaluation (ORACLE) studies (1975–80) drew attention to a dominant characteristic of primary classrooms – the 'busyness of the teacher' (Galton *et al.* 1980). The research revealed that, in general, primary teachers were engaged in some form of interaction with pupils for over 78 per cent of the time during which they were under observation. Over 70 per cent of these observed interactions were with individual pupils and just under 20 per cent were with the whole class, leaving just under 10 per cent of observed occasions where teachers were conversing with groups. The most striking consequence of this was:

> the asymmetric nature of the primary classroom, in that the pupil's pattern of interaction was almost the reverse of that of the teacher. Whereas the teacher was observed interacting with pupils for around 80 per cent of the time, the pupil, in turn, was observed interacting neither with the teacher nor with other pupils for approximately the same proportion of time when they were under observation.
>
> (Galton 1989: 45)

Three-quarters of the teacher attention that an individual pupil received was when the teacher was addressing the class, but teachers only did this for around 20 per cent of their time. Nor did the data show that pupils' lack of teacher interaction was compensated for by discussion with their peers. Such discussion only accounted for 20 per cent of the 80 per cent of time when the pupil was not involved with the teacher and nearly two-thirds of that 20 per cent of time was spent on non-task-related exchanges. A further important consequence of pupils working individually was that the tasks they were set had to be ones which could be carried out without making too many demands on the teacher. This led to increasing reliance on the use of worksheets and published schemes of work.

These findings were confirmed by the classroom data collected by Mortimore *et al.* (1988) who carried out a longitudinal study of 2,000 junior school children in 50 schools to investigate the factors contributing to effective schools. The amount of time a teacher spent interacting with the children as a whole class was found to have a significant positive relationship with progress in a wide range of areas. However, it was 'the proportion of interactions involving the class, rather than any attempt to teach the whole class as one unit, that seems to have been associated with beneficial effects' (p. 228). Although children might be working individually or engaged in some form of group work, some teachers 'more frequently introduced topics to the whole class, entered into discussions with them, and made teaching points to everyone' (p. 228). It was these kinds of interactions that appeared to be effective in promoting pupil learning.

The PNP evaluation (Alexander 1992) also examined the nature of teacher–pupil interactions. These were classified into five categories: work, monitoring, routine, disciplinary and other. As the number of routine interactions was the same as those related to work, Alexander (1992) suggested that teachers should become aware of the frequency and proportion of their range of interactions in order to make best use of the limited time available for interacting with each pupil. He also stressed the need to examine the quality of these interactions, especially teacher questions. Although teachers asked a great many questions, the potential of questioning as a teaching strategy was not fully realized because 'questions might feature as little more than conversational or rhetorical devices; they might be more token than genuine; they might be predominantly closed; and they might lack cognitive challenge' (p. 77). Three studies of questioning in the Leverhulme project (Wragg 1993) came up with similar findings including examples of the ways in which teachers, who were skilful communicators, were able to raise the level of pupils' thinking, reflection and practical activity. The project also studied teachers' explanations in different kinds of lessons and identified features which made these explanations particularly clear, helpful and stimulating. As the project was not only a research project but also one geared to contribute to teacher professional development, it produced a series of workbooks which included one on questioning (Brown and Wragg 1993) and one on explaining (Wragg and Brown 1993). These can be used by individual teachers or form the focus of school-based INSET. Consequently it is extremely worth while to devote some school-based INSET time to the examination and discussion of these issues.

Working cooperatively in groups

Another important finding of the ORACLE research was that although pupils frequently sat in groups they seldom worked cooperatively (Tann 1981). A survey by the observers of the incidence of children working in groups on a common task revealed that 69 per cent of the teachers in the sample never used cooperative group work for either art and craft or topic work and nearly 90 per cent never did so with single subject teaching such as language and mathematics. This finding was replicated in both the ILEA study (Mortimore *et al.* 1988) and the PNP evaluation (Alexander 1992) and is reflected in our own study. Insights into why group work was not often used were given by the ORACLE teachers:

the problems identified related to fears about how to manage peer groups in terms of possible noise and distraction, what size groups to use and what tasks were suitable. Also doubts were expressed about what the supposed benefits of groupwork really were and therefore what the children might be learning. Finally, there were reservations about how groupwork could be monitored.

(Tann 1988: 158)

Bennett and Dunne (1992) mount a theoretical justification for group work and review the findings of research, which has mainly been carried out in North America, revealing the gains in intellectual, social and affective development accomplished by the use of cooperative group work. As will be discussed in the next chapter in relation to achieving a balance of activities in National Curriculum planning, the PNP evaluation found that cooperative tasks involving interaction with peers and adults keep children's attention more effectively than solitary tasks. Other advantages of working together in small groups, identified by Reid *et al.* (1989), are that children can:

- generate more ideas in a collaborative setting;
- explain, question and learn from each other using the language and patterns of interaction with which they are most familiar;
- recognize the value of their own experience in acquiring and developing new knowledge;
- develop confidence in themselves as learners and in sharing ideas with a critical audience;
- develop an awareness of the differences between exploratory talk and an oral presentation;
- generate feelings of responsibility to the group and encourage self-discipline.

Bennett and Dunne (1992) worked with 15 primary teachers, who had no prior experience of cooperative group work, to gain a deeper understanding of the processes involved and the implications for classroom management, training children in group work skills and assessment of group work. A major finding in the current context of increased demands being placed on classteachers was that cooperative group work could contribute to the more effective use of teacher time. Within each group, instead of asking the teacher, children took responsibility for providing reassurance, monitoring the correctness or quality of each other's work and making decisions about the sequence of task activities, use of materials and forms of presentation of task outcomes. This released a considerable amount of teacher time for interacting with the groups, monitoring their work and carrying out formative assessment. Funded research specifically on the advantages and disadvantages of alternative kinds of group work in British primary schools is rare, although teacher researchers have explored its demands and possibilities, especially in relation to pupils' communication and social skills (see, for example, Prisk 1987; Winter 1990; Horbury and Pears 1994).

Reflecting the ORACLE data Bennett and Dunne (1992) found that for teachers one of the most difficult aspects of implementing group work was designing appropriate tasks. They identified four key features of task design which affect the cognitive demand of tasks, the ways in which children tackle their work and the nature of their talk. These may prove useful in reviewing and extending the kinds of tasks provided:

(a) The form of the task (that is, whether it is a 'production' or a 'discussion' activity) is clearly a major distinction and dominates the task design and the pupil's response; underlying this distinction is the suggestion that groupwork is dependent on problem-solving activity.
(b) The extent to which an activity contains a problem-solving element and the ways this is set up so that children recognise the problem, whether or not there is a correct 'end-product', and what 'decisions' need to be taken.
(c) The framework of the task, which can be conceived in terms of 'looseness' or 'tightness'; that is, the extent to which possibilities are widened or narrowed by the task content and instructions.
(d) Whether or not a pupil-planning stage is required as a prerequisite to further activity.

(Bennett and Dunne 1992: 89–90)

As well as examining the cognitive demands of group work Bennett and Dunne (1992) looked at different kinds of cooperative endeavour and the effect of these on the social demands made. They identified three models of cooperative task:

1 Children work individually on identical tasks for individual products, but are asked to talk to each other about their work, to help each other, thereby establishing cooperative endeavour.
2 Children work individually on 'jigsaw' elements of a task, so that a certain amount of cooperation is built into the task, especially in terms of planning and organisation.
3 Children work jointly on one task for a joint outcome, so that cooperation is of paramount importance.

(p. 91)

The description given earlier of children working together to test the resistance of various barriers is an example of the latter model. An example of the 'jigsaw' model is included in NCC's INSET video 'Working Together: English in the National Curriculum in Key Stages 1 and 2' which shows children in expert roles such as editors, writers and illustrators contributing in groups to the production of a book.

Reid *et al.* (1989: 30–31) argue that the optimum size of groups is four because:

> All students can be seated facing each other, yet no student need have her or his back to the board or to the teacher when the teacher is at the front of the room. Four seems to be the optimum number that allows for a good range of experience in the group, as well as for individual contributions. Within larger groups, the contributions of quieter members may be overlooked.

They suggest that when children have completed a task in 'home groups', which are generally friendship groups, they should move to 'sharing groups'. This avoids the need for reporting back to the whole class which can be boring and repetitious. 'Sharing groups' may be made up in a variety of ways, for example, putting a pair from one group with a pair from another. They might be mixed sex or single sex to contrast with the 'home groups'; they might also include both pupils who have experienced difficulties with the task and those who found it easier.

Bennett and Cass (1989) also consider the implications of group composition. They contrasted the effects of groups of three pupils of mixed ability and ability groups of high, average and low attainers working on the same task. They concluded that the high attaining children performed well irrespective of which group they were in and that the group of two low attainers and one high attainer was a more successful combination than two high attainers and a low attainer, which led to the low attainer being ignored or opting out. They therefore concluded that working in carefully chosen mixed ability groups could be beneficial for all children.

To conclude this section, drawing on the experiences of those teachers in our research who were introducing cooperative group work into their teaching repertoires, we give some suggestions on how to get started:

- Introduce small group work gradually by starting with children working in pairs.
- Initially keep group tasks relatively short and straightforward, such as brainstorming lists, predicting the end of a story and playing number games with calculators.
- Explain to pupils exactly what is expected of them in group work. Ask them to draw on their early experiences to suggest some rules to guide the conduct of group work.
- Make sure that the task is adequately resourced, with notional time allocations for different parts of the task and that pupils are clear about how they should go about achieving the intended outcomes.

- Ensure everyone has a job to do and is actively involved in contributing to the group task.
- Tape-record group work to find out exactly what is going on in the groups and use pupil self-reflections to inform your evaluation.
- Enlist other audiences for the outcomes of the group work – peers, other classes, parents and visitors – to give the task more status and purpose and to provide additional feedback.

Seating arrangements

While sitting in groups was the most common arrangement in the schools in our research, three classrooms in particular stood out. A Year 3 teacher, who often used whole class teaching, had arranged the chairs and tables into three arcs facing the blackboard. A few tables for use by groups were available at the back. A teacher of a Year 3/4 mixed age class sat them in year groups around two large tables made up of their small tables pushed together. The most unusual arrangement was adopted by the teacher of a Year 4/5/6 class in a small school whose classroom was in a large hut in the playground. The children sat in pairs in study carrels facing the wall for individual work. Areas for computer use and art and technology were permanently set out and other tables for group work were available in the centre of the classroom.

In the PNP evaluation Alexander comments on the frequently witnessed mismatch between 'the ostensibly collective strategy of grouping and the predominance of individualised work tasks' conveying the impression that 'the strategy of grouping has become an end in itself rather than a device adopted for particular educational purposes' (1992: 67). This impression was heightened by data gathered in a national sample of classrooms as part of another project based at Leeds University – the SEAC-funded evaluation of the 1991 KS1 National Assessment. These national data suggested a further mismatch, 'between this same collaborative setting and the teacher's predominantly individual or whole class mode of interaction' (Alexander 1992: 67).

Two small studies (Hastings and Schwieso 1994) challenged the apparent orthodoxy of sitting in groups and investigated the relationship of task requirements to two seating arrangements – groups and rows. They found that the most readily distracted children concentrated better on their individual work – often set in English and mathematics – when seated in rows. They advocate that children learn two or three basic arrangements of the furniture and move it to suit the learning activity. They suggest that the time taken in doing this should be more than compensated for by the quality and quantity of work and increased time on task. While the upheaval of moving furniture around in overcrowded classrooms can be considerable, alternative arrangements might be adopted when longer blocks of time than single lessons are given to activities. Also shared areas might be set out in a variety of ways to provide those children using them with greater diversity of seating.

McNamara (1994) suggests a possible solution to being able to move readily into different forms of classroom organization is to have a basic arrangement of the desks in a horseshoe. This involves arranging the desks around the sides of the classroom with children facing into the middle, thus enabling the teacher to see every child and every child to see the teacher during class lessons. He identifies the following advantages of this arrangement:

● Children can see each other and are more inclined to listen to each other's contributions than when seated in rows with their backs to colleagues, or in groups where eye contact and audibility are difficult.
● A large space is available in the middle of the room for stories, large pieces of artwork and so on.
● Children are able, when required, to work in pairs or threes, that is group sizes which are productive and unlikely to exclude people. (Often group size is determined by the number of children who can sit around table arrangements, rather than educational considerations.)
● The teacher can see, at a glance, what every child is doing and reach those with problems quickly.
● Desks can quickly be formed into tables of four when required.

(McNamara 1994: 66)

Ability grouping, setting and streaming

In the majority of classes children sat in friendship groups, although some children were repositioned by the teacher away from their closest friends to control off-task or disruptive behaviour. Usually, once children had chosen a place, they had to stay there for at least half a term or a term. In mixed age classes the children were usually divided into age groups within which they sat in friendship groups.

Children were frequently grouped by ability in mathematics and this determined where they were on the school mathematics scheme and/or the nature and level of the work that they were given. However, they only sat or worked together in such ability groups when they were given specific individual or cooperative group tasks or the teacher taught them as a distinct group. An example of an exception to this was a Year 4/5 teacher who organized his class in five groups of six children according to mathematical ability. He used the groups, which he reviewed each half term, for some activities other than mathematics. Throughout the sample children were also often grouped according to ability in English. As with the mathematics groups, while this influenced the work that they were given, only occasionally did they either sit or work together in ability groups.

A few schools made limited use of setting. For example, in a 9–13 middle school the decision to have three ability groups for French had resulted in a knock-on effect leading to ability grouping in mathematics and science. The headteacher explained that they were against ability grouping for English because it was taught largely through literature appreciation, and an awareness of the issues dealt with and an aptitude for literary criticism were not necessarily linked to the more academic English language skills.

In a large primary school with mixed age and mixed key stage classes the teachers were experimenting with setting across the three Year 6 classes for mathematics and English in order both to cater better for children's learning needs and to prepare them for secondary school. Two part time teachers were used to create additional groups and to make the setting more effective. When the year group was set for English, one part time teacher took a group of 12 children – four lower-ability pupils from each class – for special help. When the year group was set for mathematics, the involvement of the other part time teacher meant that the mathematics specialist in the year group could take a small group of able children and give them more demanding work. For an hour each day for four days mathematics was taught in sets and for the fifth day teachers took their own classes for mathematics so they could see what the children were doing, since it was they who needed to fill their records in. A constraint on the use of setting was that it required those classes involved to work to a shared timetable. While this was readily achieved in mathematics, which tended to take place during the first session in the morning, it was thought preferable to keep the timing of other subjects flexible so they could be taught in a range of ways, including through topic work and a menu approach. Until the 1980s there had been streaming in the school based on attainment in English. This had been experienced by the deputy headteacher who had been at the school for 20 years:

> For the very bright it worked; for the least able, it partly worked; I don't think it did anything for the middle at all; I don't think socially it was any good. I started here and was given the top year D class, remedial class you know, of 20, and I see them now as 30-year-olds holding down responsible jobs and so on. They weren't remedial children, they shouldn't have been stigmatized as such – many of them – and they were only remedial in our terms anyway.

Most teachers made some use of ability grouping within their own classes and, where it would be feasible, appeared willing to try out some setting in the core subjects. However streaming was viewed as an unjust system which both took minimal account of the fact that children often performed at different levels in different subjects and damaged their self-image at a very early age by labelling them as failures – a view shared by those researchers who have studied the effects of streaming in primary schools (see, for example, Jackson 1964). We found no teachers who supported streaming.

Differentiation

Since the introduction of the National Curriculum the term differentiation – often undefined and open to a range of interpretations – has appeared increasingly in policy documents at national, local and school level. Below are three definitions which we have found helpful and which in combination outline the main characteristics and purposes of differentiation:

> By differentiation is meant the identification of, and effective provision for, a range of abilities in one classroom, such that pupils in a particular class need not study the same things at the same pace and in the same way at all times. Differentiated approaches should mean that the needs of the very able, and of children with learning difficulties, are discerned and met.
>
> (Scottish Education Department, quoted in Simpson 1989: 73)

> • enabling pupils of different backgrounds and abilities to demonstrate what they know, understand and are able to do;
> • ensuring that pupils are given tasks which are commensurate with their level of attainment;
> • ensuring that pupils achieve success and feel that learning experiences have been worthwhile.
>
> (DES, quoted in J. Moore 1992: 16)

> Differentiation is therefore seen as the process of identifying, with each learner, the most effective strategies for achieving agreed targets.
>
> (Weston 1992: 6)

As the overwhelming majority of primary school classes are mixed ability, teachers have always recognized the importance of providing a diversity of learning activities to meet the different learning needs of pupils. However, getting the correct match between the intellectual, manual and affective demand of tasks and pupils' abilities has proved difficult in practice for even those teachers recognized as being particularly effective (see for example, Bennett *et al.* 1984; Simpson 1989). The introduction of the National Curriculum and its associated assessment were viewed as likely to improve differentiation by increasing teachers' awareness of the level of attainment of individuals in each subject and providing a 10-level framework within which to plan for progression. However in a 1990 conference address Richards, when reflecting on data collected on the early implementation of the National Curriculum through HMI inspections, reports:

> Differentiation of work continues to be a thorny and, in one sense, an insoluble problem. It is a pipedream, it is an impossible goal to differentiate work to suit the individual pupils' needs across the range of the curriculum. Nevertheless, steps can be taken to improve, to some degree or another, differentiation of work, even if within the limits of the possible rather than the desirable.
>
> (reported by Campbell 1991: 11)

Desforges (1985: 102) in an analysis of why differentiation appears an insoluble problem concludes that:

> Indeed it might be that the classroom as presently conceived has reached levels of productivity, in terms of learning outcomes and happy relationships, consistent with its design limitations. Improvements might require radical reconceptions of teaching and learning situations.

This view was supported by the teachers with whom Simpson (1989) worked: 'given the number of children, given the curriculum, given the range of demands and constraints, the matching is as good as we can make it' (p. 88). The intractable difficulties inherent in the process of differentiation have to be acknowledged, but we should not be self-defeating. Differentiation can increase pupil understanding, motivation, enjoyment and confidence in learning. Therefore, as Richards suggests, it is important to look for ways forward to effect improvements.

Our data reveal how differentiation was being tackled in the sample schools and provides ideas as to how the aspirations in the opening quotations might be realized. A junior school teacher explained how she catered for the differences in ability of the pupils in her class:

> I tend to plan work for the class as a whole and then have to adapt it . . . so like today we're doing work on volume and they've already finished their work so I'll have to get extra work to stretch them a bit further – extension workcards or another activity to do or give them something completely different. With the poorer ones, perhaps I'll allow them to take longer, or I will go back over it two or three times to make sure they've got it.

In common with many primary teachers she differentiated work in three main ways:

1 The provision for the able of additional more demanding work in the same area once they had completed that set for the class.
2 The allocation of completely different activities for pupils of different abilities.
3 Setting the same task for all pupils but expecting a range of outcomes in terms of speed of task completion, quality and quantity of work and the amount of help required.

The time required for task completion usually appeared to be left to the individual pupils to decide. Although teachers may have had expectations as to how long individuals should need to complete work, they seldom made this explicit. Hence in several classes time spent on tasks appeared to us to be infinitely expandable, which was in sharp contrast to the teacher's perceptions of rushing through an overloaded curriculum. For example, a class was set the task of finding out information from reference books on aspects of Victorian homes in the lesson before morning break and they continued with this until lunchtime. As the task was neither broken down into component parts in order to give it a structure nor was any time limit given, it was difficult for both the teacher and the children to gauge progress. By halfway through the second lesson, while the teacher worked with a group on the task, most of the other children – having located any relevant information in the books provided – sat quietly doing very little. By contrast in a Year 4/5/6 class, where periodically the teacher stated at what point in the various tasks children should be, this appeared to increase motivation and to clarify the depth and quantity of work expected. This technique appeared extremely helpful.

Some teachers described how they catered for children of different abilities by taking the same task and modifying it. For example, a mathematics task was presented to a class in the form of a worksheet but a support teacher explained the task to two boys with learning difficulties. Other ways of enabling pupils to access the same task might be to provide it on audio tape and/or in pictorial or diagrammatic form. Another example of a modified task was in a technology lesson where all the children were asked to make the same model but were given different materials with which to construct it. As well as modifying the presentation of the task and the process involved in carrying it out, the end product or response can be differentiated through the use of alternative forms of presentation. Another way of taking into account children's interests and abilities while working within mixed ability groups, is to use the jigsaw approach to cooperative group work described earlier.

Other approaches to differentiation that were observed were:

● the use of individualized schemes, especially in mathematics and English grammar, and the use of computer programs;
● open-ended tasks allowing pupils to suggest the mode of response –

for example, asking pupils to predict the strength of a range of disposable shopping bags and devise tests to investigate their predictions;

- menu arrangements whereby pupils select tasks from a range of possibilities and complete them in the order that they prefer and at their own pace;
- supplying different degrees of teacher assistance, for example in storywriting; the provision of spellings; additional stimuli for ideas; putting the child's ideas into written sentences and the ongoing reading through together and correction of drafts;
- the production of graded tasks.

However, the production of graded tasks was viewed as a more complex approach which demanded generally too much preparation time for it to occur regularly. First, an analysis of the task into small steps was required. Second, pupils' current mastery of these steps had to be diagnosed. Third, activities had to be planned focusing on one step or combinations of these steps tailored to the diagnosed needs of individuals or groups. A simple example of this approach was the use of a set of handwriting activities and cards in a Year 3 class. Several teachers anticipated that catering for pupils' abilities and needs would gradually become easier as they repeated aspects of topics and subjects because they were building up sets of workcards and banks of resources for differentiated activities.

One way in which differentiation was indirectly aided in some classes was through teaching children to become independent self-servicing learners capable of managing and evaluating their own learning. This involved sharing the purpose behind tasks with children and helping them to understand and to contribute to the criteria by which their work would be assessed. This was achieved through, when being shown completed work, asking questions such as 'Well what do you think of it?' 'What do you like about it?' and 'How could you make it better?' Also, by giving children evaluation sheets to fill in when tasks were completed or by asking them to write about 'what went well and what did not'. For example, one teacher helped pupils to photograph their technology models and then to write an evaluation of the process of making the models and the finished product. These were then put into a class book which served as a record of their technology project.

Pupils who can sensibly and confidently exercise their own discretion and have begun to internalize standards can free teachers from routine questions and unnecessary tasks, so reducing interruptions when they are helping individuals and groups. We saw some examples of pupils taking responsibility not only for their own learning but also for the learning of others. For example, in the carousel activity described earlier in this chapter, where children were working in pairs to write poems on dragons, they were correcting each other's spelling and sentence construction. Also, in a Year 4/5/6 class in a primary school, some children were writing individual stories about a mystery object. When they had finished their first drafts, they worked in pairs and, taking it in turns, each acted as a 'critical friend' and gave advice as to how both the content and style of the story could be improved. In small schools where children of mixed age groups work together, younger and older pupils could easily be asked to work together in ways which promote their intellectual development and improve their self-image. Older children of all abilities were asked to provide explanations, assistance and resources for younger ones. The younger ones used the older ones and their work as sources of information and models for what they would be able to achieve.

Another way in which teachers achieved differentiation and additional learning opportunities, especially for pupils with special educational needs (SEN) was through the use of part time staff, NTAs and volunteer helpers. A teacher of a Year 2/3 class explained how she used her additional classroom help:

We have a .5 teacher that we share. I have her Monday mornings for an hour. How I use her is up to me. I give her a group of six top infants and she works with them. I have her also for withdrawal when she takes out the child in the top infants who needs statementing. We have an NTA who is shared out. On Monday I have her for an hour at the end of the afternoon, where she can't possibly help with children, and so I use her for resources, and so, the language sheets that I devise as coordinator which need photocopying, I use her for that. Wednesday morning I have her for an hour and so I tend to use her working with a group. I like to team teach and so if I am coping with one group I will give her another to supervise. I have a mum, who comes in all Tuesday morning . . . who listens to reading, and I have a grandma, who comes in Wednesday morning and also listens to reading, and occasionally a grandparent comes in Wednesday afternoon. I tend to use them as backup for reading as that's the one problem in practice – listening to people read.

This Year 2/3 teacher had no non-contact time because she chose to use the part time teacher, who was timetabled to relieve her, to provide extra help for a child with learning difficulties. Several classteachers in the sample chose to relinquish their non-contact time in order to enable another teacher to work with an individual or group of children with special needs or to do so themselves.

In several of the sample schools parents and other volunteer helpers were observed assisting in the classroom with a range of activities. While schools found their help invaluable, the planning and organizing of such contributions and managing personal relationships makes additional demands on classteachers, as documented by Tricker (1992). The majority of the schools employed NTAs which, as Mortimore and Mortimore (1992) have pointed out, have the potential to make cost-effective and important contributions by substituting for part of a teacher's role and augmenting some activities. However, the limited number of hours for which most of them were employed, the ways in which their time was fragmented because it was shared out among staff, and the fact that in primary schools they generally spent most of their time with the KS1 children, limited the contribution that they were able to make to the work of any one KS2 teacher.

The above unsatisfactory situation is changing. Haigh (1994a: 4) reports that 'in the two years between January 1991 and 1993 the number of classroom assistants in England went up from 6,342 to 9,304'. This trend is likely to increase owing to the new £2 million programme of one-year training courses for specialist teaching assistants (STAs) instigated by the Secretary of State for Education in November 1993 and starting in 24 training institutions in autumn 1994. Schools can use their new budgetary freedom to employ more people to assist classteachers to meet the ever increasing demands made on them. However, there is a danger that constraints on budgets could lead to STAs being used inappropriately as teachers-on-the-cheap. Schools can employ two or three assistants for the cost of one teacher as salary levels are low. Annual pay in 1995 typically ranges between £3,500 and £5,500 for a 25-hour week. Unions have been cautious therefore in their approach to classroom assistants. Initially, professional boundaries may seem blurred, but such problems can be resolved by job descriptions, whole school agreements over the use of assistants and, most importantly, by classteachers and assistants working closely together and negotiating the ways in which their roles are complementary. As illustrated in an account of the use of assistants at Sutton-at-Hone Primary (Haigh 1994a), such assistants can with advice from the teacher modify materials to improve differentiation.

The proliferation of school policies, especially since the introduction of OFSTED inspections, makes us hesitant to recommend any additional ones. However, differentiation is certainly an area which demands whole school consideration in order to share and to make explicit teachers' concerns and ideas and bring together the relevant discussion and experience likely to have been derived from National Curriculum planning and assessment. A meeting, workshop or INSET session could be called to identify and consolidate what has been achieved. A starting point might be to review the teaching taking place on one afternoon and to identify ways in which teachers modified the tasks set through the presentation, accomplishment or outcome of the task and to explore additional possibilities, perhaps in relation to two particular children with learning needs. While the SEN coordinator might lead an initiative on differentiation, it is important that it does not become conceived of as solely or mainly an SEN issue.

Assessment, recording and reporting

Commenting on the detailed and prescriptive nature of the original National Curriculum Orders, Dearing (1993a: 61) acknowledges that:

> We have created an over-elaborate system which distorts the nature of the different subjects, which serves to fragment teaching and learning in that teachers are planning work from the statements of attainment, and which has at times reduced the assessment process to a meaningless ticking of myriad boxes.

Prior to the Dearing review, in order to meet statutory requirements teachers were keeping checklists of pupils' attainments in National Curriculum subjects. Some schools had devised their own checklists for ticking off the SoAs attained but most were either using the record marketed by Modbury County Primary School, other commercially produced pupil attainment records or those developed by their LEA. While most records provided a box to tick when the SoA was attained and a space for comments, some records were even more time-consuming and complex. For example, one primary teacher explained that on the tick sheet that she used, she 'put a dot when a new area was introduced, a line through when it was practised and a cross when attained'. Schools also used colour coding to show in which year an SoA was first covered. As well as maintaining records of National Curriculum attainment, some teachers also kept additional pupil records of phonic sheets completed, books read from reading schemes, fiction read, scores in mental arithmetic tests, and activities undertaken in topic or subject areas.

Many teachers questioned the validity and therefore the value of the attainment records for the following reasons:

● teachers were interpreting the SoAs differently;
● teachers were uncertain of exactly what was required at each level;
● children often did not retain the skills and knowledge that they demonstrated at the time of the assessment;
● many teachers, especially in KS2, had had no training in techniques for assessment;
● most teachers had no opportunities to engage in moderation activities.

Some teachers were concerned that National Curriculum assessment, which they perceived as 'trying to tie kids down into categories', might lead to children being labelled in ways which would predetermine teachers' expectations of them:

Assessment seems to have come full circle. At my first school, children were referred to as A children, B children, C children. Now it's levels 1, 2, 3 and I wonder if that's a retrograde step. Are we going to categorize children? 'Oh he is a level 4 child, he should be better than that. Oh he's only level 2, no wonder he behaves like that' – and these kind of stereotypes. I fear that.

Other teachers were also worried about the pressure 'to push children towards level 5' because of the publication of SAT league tables. They wondered whether this might result in 'cheating' by some teachers.

The ongoing changes to the National Curriculum subjects, which meant existing assessment records were a 'mishmash' of old and new, had involved teachers in considerable extra work to update records and caused schools to incur additional expenses through having to purchase more paper and record books. This served to undermine the usefulness and credibility of the assessment and recording processes:

You're just living from day to day, and you just assume all your records are now going to be changed. You've had the stuffing knocked out of you . . . When they first came in you made a real decided effort to come to terms with it and get it all right. You had your planning and you had your records. The LEA have changed the records twice since then. I mean they've changed the National Curriculum I don't know how many times. They've changed SATs every time they've come out, so now I mean you just don't believe it any more. So you just think, 'Right, I don't believe it, I'll just tick along today, because tomorrow it will be different'.

As this book demonstrates, the seemingly never ending stream of requirements from central government meant that all schools had to face competing priorities and for only some was producing an assessment policy and setting up effective systems to implement it top of the list. To meet their statutory obligations schools often introduced new assessment practices before teachers had had the opportunity to share and reflect on existing school procedures and develop a whole school policy. As shown in the quotation above, practices tended to be reactive and changed on the basis of new demands, as opposed to being informed by reflection and evaluation. Curriculum coordinators often provided assistance with assessment in their subjects, which sometimes involved staff meetings to compare judgements on pieces of work. However, the responsibility for bringing together approaches to the various aspects of assessment across the school, using these as a basis for writing a draft policy for discussion and identifying ways forward was usually the responsibility of assessment coordinators.

In the majority of schools, judgements about individual attainment were reached through observing and questioning pupils while they worked, short tests given to the whole class and from written work. However, increasingly teachers were starting to incorporate tasks specifically for assessment purposes into their short term plans. For example, a Year 5 class in a middle school was doing a project on Egypt and in order to test pupils' skills in deduction their teacher had planned an oral assessment task whereby they selected one of a range of postcards on tomb paintings and responded to the following questions: first, 'What is happening in the painting and what does it tell you about Egyptian life?' (AT3, use of historical sources, level 3: make deductions from historical sources); second, 'Why might what you say about the picture be different from what someone else says about the same picture?' (AT2 interpretations of history, level 4: show an understanding that deficiencies in evidence may lead to different interpretations). If such oral assessments were to be conducted smoothly and effectively by the teacher without any assistance, classes needed to be well managed. Some teachers were concerned that while they were carrying out such assessments other pupils had to do less demanding tasks for which they did not need assistance. The objectives upon which assessment tasks were based were usually taken from the SoAs. Consequently teachers were uncertain as to how they would arrive at the focus of such tasks once the SoAs were replaced by level descriptions and whether it might be useful to retain the original orders for help in assessment planning where parts of the PoS had not changed substantially.

A few schools had well established records of achievement (RoAs) which usually had their origins in work prior to the introduction of the National Curriculum. These were highly valued for their contribution to pupil motivation and for encouraging pupils to better understand, and to take responsibility for, their own learning. Other schools were at various stages in the process of developing such RoAs. The RoA folder in one primary school typified that towards which schools were working. It consisted of five sections:

1 formal personal records;
2 records of pupils' personal and social skills, interests, activities and achievements within and outside school;
3 National Curriculum attainment record, test scores, SAT results and diagnostic information;

4 reports to parents, pupil self-assessments and records of meetings between pupil and teacher in order to review work;
5 examples of work and evidence of achievement.

In addition to, and in support of, each child's RoA was a portfolio containing samples of work in the core subjects. Two samples from each core subject were selected once a term and were annotated by both the teacher and the child as to why that particular piece of work was chosen. At the end of the year the teacher and the child agreed on two pieces of work from each subject to go into the child's RoA. While this school had a clear whole school policy about the aims, objectives and processes involved in compiling an RoA, other schools were still awaiting the opportunity to make use of a school training day to begin to develop such a policy. The amount of work that should be kept in a pupil's portfolio was an issue in a number of schools, although most admitted that, while initially they had tended to collect far too much, they were now becoming increasingly selective.

As in the above example, several schools were concerned to involve pupils in the self-assessment of activities and in the compilation of their RoAs in the kinds of ways suggested by Emery (1996). For example, one primary school gave children a book each year in which they recorded the work done in the core subjects, technology, history and geography throughout each week. On Friday they identified and wrote comments on those lessons that they had particularly enjoyed or ones in which they felt that they had learned the most. These books, together with the ongoing work in pupils' drawers, formed the basis for twice-yearly interviews with parents at which the child was present and targets were identified for the next six months. In a middle school, which operated a profiling system derived from a pyramid project to look at assessment and profiling from 4–19 years, staff were reviewing the children's contributions in order to reduce staff workloads and to better meet National Curriculum requirements. Originally the children had selected the work to go into the portfolio and the teacher had annotated it retrospectively with the context in which it was produced and the reason for its retention. Now the teachers were devising tasks in each subject – with the exception of PE and music – which would produce evidence of National Curriculum attainment. When they set the task they gave the children criteria, referred to as 'points to remember', against which to assess their performance. Following the children's assessment, the teacher then supplied overall comments. In this way a wallet of subject profiles was built up for each child.

The research across 13 LEAs revealed that, at any point in time, while each school had its own particular priorities, the same concerns derived from national advice or the latest legislation could suddenly sweep across schools and assessment was an area in which this was very noticeable. Hence at the beginning of the first phase schools were devising records of National Curriculum attainment. At the end of this phase filing cabinets were being delivered into classrooms as the compilation of individual portfolios got underway. Towards the end of the second phase of fieldwork, schools felt under pressure to have a school assessment portfolio containing agreed levels of work produced by children in the school. Advice from LEAs advocated the value of these:

- to standardize levels awarded by teachers within schools;
- as evidence of the ability of teachers to make consistent accurate assessments for audit moderators to look at;
- as a source of reference for beginning teachers, supply teachers, governors and parents;
- and to limit the amount of evidence necessary to demonstrate the performance of individuals.

Schools that had already put a great deal of time and effort into establishing an effective assessment system, which had involved school-based agreement trials and the development of individual pupil portfolios, were in the strongest position to compile such a portfolio. In most schools, with the exception of those KS1 teachers who had undergone LEA agreement trial training and participated in assessment moderation, the majority of teachers, who had not received relevant training, appeared to be very unclear as to the purposes, other than in relation to accountability, of school portfolios. Thus they were unsure as to what might be involved in producing and using them and did not recognize that, rather than a task to be completed, portfolios should be regarded as ongoing with material added and deleted over time. However, with proper organization and adequate external support, as demonstrated by Conner (1994) and Clarke and Christie (1995), the debates generated by agreement trialing and the compilation of school portfolios provide an excellent professional development opportunity focusing on teaching and learning.

Most schools had devised an annual report for parents based on DES guidelines or were using a report form issued by their LEA. The introduction of formal written end-of-year reports into schools, where they had not previously existed or had only consisted of general comments or selective points of praise or concern, contributed to the burden of additional work. One school, which was in its third year of operating a system of reporting to parents through meetings based on pupils' RoAs, was continuing with this in preference to sending home an annual report. The head explained how it operated:

> We have our own profiling system where each child in turn has an individual time with the teacher. It's built into the school day . . .

The parent comes in for an individual appointment – 20 minutes at the minimum – and goes through the work and talks about anything. Then we have a sort of sheet which summarizes the discussion and the parent signs it and the teacher signs it and the child signs it – if the child has been involved, which we encourage. That is an ongoing thing. Every term, every week, parents are coming in, children are being profiled and it rolls on built into the teacher's day – and most parents get three interviews a year.

The school had the support of its governors and parents as a result of a period of consultation during which parents completed a pro forma evaluating the system and stating whether it should be continued.

The escalating workloads necessary to meet the demands of assessment, recording and reporting prior to the Dearing review were taking their toll of teachers' energy, job satisfaction and confidence. Nevertheless, teachers identified a number of advantages arising out of their work on assessment. They considered that they were more aware of their pupils' progress and their strengths and weaknesses in particular aspects of subjects. Also, teachers felt that pupils were often clearer about the goals and purposes of their work and the criteria by which it was judged and some teachers were devising imaginative ways of involving pupils in the assessment process. The lack of funds for assessment training and moderation activities and the nature of the tests at KS2 and their external marking are all important factors constraining the development of teacher expertise in assessment. However, the moratorium on curriculum change may enable teachers to review, share and consolidate what they have achieved and continue to improve school assessment practices.

three

Changing curriculum organization and planning

The most immediate requirement with the publication of the orders for the core subjects was for schools to engage in a process of curriculum audit and planning on an unprecedented scale. This was ongoing through the introduction of the foundation subjects and is continuing with the publication of the revised orders in January 1995. This chapter focuses on the planning demands and the issues in relation to curriculum organization generated by the introduction of the National Curriculum. It opens by reviewing the impact of the National Curriculum on topic work which was initially envisaged by teachers as the main vehicle for combining and covering the attainment targets (ATs). This is followed by consideration of how the 9-subject curriculum (now 10, with technology and IT as separate subjects), plus religious education (RE) is making enormous additional demands on teachers in terms of subject knowledge, familiarity with National Curriculum requirements and expertise in utilizing subject knowledge in the teaching of pupils. The DES discussion paper (Alexander *et al.* 1992) suggests that in order to meet these demands schools are likely to introduce more separate subject teaching – a message reiterated in subsequent publications from policy makers (for example, NCC 1993a; OFSTED 1993a). However, expectations that classteachers should develop an allegiance to one or more subjects in addition to their concern for the children in their class is a new departure for many teachers. We draw on the project data to examine some of the ways in which schools are making greater use of teachers' subject expertise and the teachers' perceptions of their associated benefits and limitations.

Advice at national and LEA level has consistently exhorted teachers to take account in their National Curriculum planning of breadth and balance, progression and continuity. As argued by Kelly and Blenkin

(1993), these terms, which are generally undefined, have become overused unquestioned rhetorical devices at all levels of policy making. They consider 'breadthandbalance', as they put it, to be particularly problematic because of the way in which the two terms have been conflated into a single notion containing the assumption that breadth entails balance and vice versa. The final part of this chapter discusses these terms and looks at the planning issues that they pose for teachers.

Topic work and the introduction of the National Curriculum

Topic work has been a major feature in primary education for the last two decades (for discussion of its origins, nature and popularity, see for example, Conner 1988; Kerry and Eggleston 1988; Tann 1988). As well as being known by a range of labels – project, thematic work, centre of interest, humanities and environmental studies – topic work is open to multiple interpretations which makes its prevalence difficult to quantify. However, Alexander *et al.* (1992: 21) suggest that:

> About 30 per cent of work in primary schools is taught as single subjects. Music, physical education, most mathematics and some English are usually taught as separate subjects. The other foundation subjects are very often taught, entirely or largely, as aspects of topic work.

Alexander *et al.* (1992: 21) define a topic as 'a mode of curriculum organisation, frequently enquiry based, which brings elements of different subjects together under a common theme'. In this definition subject integration is the key characteristic of topic work. However, for Alexander (1988: 154) topic work together with the integrated day and group work is part of 'an interconnected package or edifice of ideas, practices, institutions and roles' derived from 'progressive' primary education which are espoused through 'Primaryspeak' (the vague undefined language of liberal progressive education). The definition provided by ATL (AMMA 1992: 12) emphasizes the contribution to topic work of enquiry-based teaching but divorces it from any particular form of curriculum organization:

> Topic work is a method of organising learning involving enquiry. It can be used to deliver material in a separate subject (for example, a science topic such as mini-beasts) or themes in which a number of subjects are integrated (for example, a topic on Voyages of Discovery in which aspects of history, geography, technology and English are involved). Teaching through integrated topics or

through single subjects can be done both effectively and ineffectively, for their success depends primarily on the quality of the planning and teaching, not on the curriculum structure.

The HMI series on 'Aspects of Primary Education' provides descriptions of successful topics taught both within and across subjects and serves to illustrate both the ambiguous umbrella nature of the term and ATL's point that the effectiveness of topics is dependent upon the quality of the teaching. For example, the case studies of effective practice in history and geography include a history-focused topic on an abandoned lead mining village, a broad-based topic on the interrelationship between people and their environment and a village study using drama to promote historical and geographical investigation (DES 1989b).

The introduction of a subject-based National Curriculum for primary schools, which came on stream one subject at a time, appeared to pose a threat to topic work. However, teachers could gain reassurance from *A Framework for the Primary Curriculum* (NCC 1989: 7) which recognized that 'in primary schools a range of work takes place which is described as "thematic", "topic-based" or "cross-curricular" in nature' and that it would therefore 'be counter-productive to lose existing good practice and unhelpful for the learner to devise an unnecessarily fragmented curriculum'. This message was reinforced by *Curriculum Guidance 3* (NCC 1990c: 1) which asserted that 'in due course, it is likely that schools will "throw all the attainment targets in a heap on the floor and reassemble them in a way which provides for them the very basis of a whole curriculum"'. The examples of topic work in NCC's non-statutory guidance (NSG) and guidance on the cross-curricular themes (see for example *Education for Economic and Industrial Understanding*; NCC 1990a) further led teachers to believe that the National Curriculum documents supported a topic approach.

However, criticisms of topic work raised in HMI reports over the last decade that much of it 'is very undemanding', 'amounts to little more than aimless and superficial copying from books' and lacks 'progression' were reiterated in the DES discussion paper (Alexander *et al*. 1992: 22). The OFSTED (1993a: 8) follow-up to the paper reported that 'the vast majority of primary schools remain firmly committed to grouping aspects of various subjects together to be taught as "topics"' although there was 'a noticeable shift towards designing topics that were more focused on a single subject'. The report states that 'about two-thirds of the schools had a satisfactory balance between topics and separate subjects but where the balance was unsatisfactory, it usually erred in the direction of an over-reliance on topics' (OFSTED 1993a: 8). In the NCC's advice to the Secretary of State for Education (1993a) on the steps considered necessary to achieve the objectives of the ERA, the Council is in no doubt that 'some of the problems encountered by schools in managing the National Curriculum are rooted in adherence to pre-National Curriculum approaches to curriculum organisation and teaching methodology' (p. 12). Consequently, they recommend 'that serious and urgent attention should be given to the greater use of single-subject teaching and of subject teachers' (p. 13).

During the initial phase of the fieldwork (autumn 1992–spring 1993) the majority of planning was topic focused. Most schools had kept a number of existing topics because they were considered successful, were well resourced and often made use of the locality or established fieldtrips. In order to establish how much of the National Curriculum such topics covered these were analysed in terms of the PoS and ATs – especially the latter. Most schools planned for six topics a year (one per half a term) although, as one head explained, an advantage of only having three topics a year was that it created space to carry out an analysis of what had actually been achieved and enabled the 'gaps' to be plugged. When gaps were identified the topic was modified to accommodate the missing subject matter and, if this was not possible without making superficial or meaningless links, then the gaps were covered in mini-topics and specific subject lessons. This process occurred both at the planning stage of a topic and at the end when pupil records of subject coverage were compared with the intentions specified in plans. As one headteacher put it:

> Planning isn't growing out of what you've done, which is the way you used to do it. Now, it's growing out of what you haven't done. You've got a hole there and you think, 'Oh I haven't covered anything on "materials" this year, so right I've got to plug a gap. I'll have to do a science topic on materials' . . . What you shouldn't do is teach to the ATs, but you do, because you teach to the gaps in your records.

For Stannard (1995), one of Her Majesty's Inspectors, one of the main problems of managing the curriculum through topics is their potentially limitless and overambitious nature which can all too readily lead to 'drift, as work planned for one subject, e.g. science, is allowed to shift into another, e.g. creative writing, drawing etc.' (p. 4). The majority of teachers agreed that planning for National Curriculum implementation had resulted in topics being much more carefully thought through and rigorous and considered that, because of this, problems such as 'drift' were beginning to be acknowledged and addressed:

> Before you didn't plan in the same detail that we plan now. I'm much more conscious of getting the balance between subjects – before it would have been almost incidental. We use the programmes of study – I don't start with the ATs. The problem with topics is that you have to decide what to leave out – perhaps we

weren't selective enough before – otherwise it's like Topsy, it can grow and grow. That's why planning is so important, to have in your mind the areas of the curriculum that you want to cover and not to get sidetracked.

While in some schools topics included a range of subjects, pressure from the policy makers at national level together with the practical problems of trying to implement and assess a vastly overloaded National Curriculum increasingly pushed teachers towards subject-focused topics and subject teaching.

Our current research in six case study schools suggests that topic work continues to remain popular. A school curriculum whereby all subjects and aspects of subjects are variously taught through separate subject teaching and topics would seem the best way forward in order to exploit the advantages of both approaches. While acknowledging the weaknesses of poorly planned topics, which can lead to a poor standard of work, as argued by Woods (1993: 5) 'this does not justify the stampede to traditionalism, wherein much excellent work is being squeezed out'. His study of critical events in teaching and learning include: primary children writing a noted children's book (*Rushavenn Time*); the making of a film of a village community (Laxfield, Suffolk); the design of a heritage centre in Winchester; and an archaeological project on a Romano–British site in south London. While few primary school topics prove as exceptional as those events portrayed by Woods, they are clearly of the same genre and share similar characteristics and possibilities for pupil motivation and learning. It is therefore important that topic work in primary schools is retained and developed. The following questions focus on issues and criticisms which are often raised in relation to teaching through topics. This checklist could be used when reviewing or formulating a school policy on the purpose and use of topic work and/or designing a topic:

- Have staff agreed on the aims, intentions and purposes of topic teaching?
- What criteria are used to decide when and which subjects or aspects of subjects are taught through topics?
- Does the balance of subject elements in the topics over the year/key stage meet National Curriculum requirements and the school's intentions?
- Are there lessons within a topic which address specific aspects of subjects?
- Are the key characteristics of each subject – concepts, skills, language – taught adequately?
- Is there an opportunity for pupils to contribute their own ideas to the direction or content of the topic?

- How is progression within particular subjects maintained from one topic to another?
- How is pupil progress in the subject elements monitored?
- How are topics evaluated?

Teachers' subject knowledge

The introduction of the National Curriculum has made heavy demands on teachers' subject knowledge which have only been marginally reduced by the slimming down of the curriculum in the 1995 orders. Following the Dearing review, Richards (1994) calls for 'the professional honesty which has acknowledged the necessary limitations of the "all-purpose, all-providing" generalist teacher' to be retained. He advises that: 'In catching their breath, all primary schools should keep their staff deployment options open – and all, except for one-teacher schools, have some options' (p. 9).

There is a growing body of evidence, which is reviewed in Bennett *et al.* (1994), to support the claim that teachers' subject knowledge is directly related to their competency to teach that subject and the quality of pupils' learning. As identified by Shulman (1986, 1987), this knowledge includes not only the basic concepts, principles and procedures of the discipline but also pedagogical content knowledge which includes ways of representing the subject to others through explanations, analogies, illustrations, examples and demonstrations. Furthermore, evidence from the evaluation of the PNP project (Alexander 1992) suggests that lack of subject knowledge may also have a negative influence on teachers' generic skills. Alexander speculates that insufficiently challenging tasks and teachers' use of unfocused questions and indiscriminate praise may be 'camouflaging' devices which serve to disguise 'the extent to which a classteacher's limited grasp of specialist subject matter may make unavailable the options of adopting a more focused and challenging mode of questioning, or making judicious use of a didactic mode' (p. 80). Consequently, he concludes that 'one of the preconditions for productive teacher–pupil interaction, therefore, must be curriculum mastery on the part of the teacher: keeping one step (or one SoA) ahead of the children is not enough' (p .81).

As the order for each National Curriculum subject was published, it was usually the focus of whole school discussions to review existing practice and for teachers to share their anxieties, strengths and ideas and familiarize themselves with the new requirements. As one teacher described it:

> I know generally in this school music and PE and drama are subjects
> that people don't feel very happy about. We've tended to focus

down on a particular subject area as a school and because we've done that people have developed more confidence. As each new area comes in, we tended to look at that and people tend to be OK after a while, once they've actually planned a topic and had a go at it.

Also, as discussed in Chapter 4, one of the main contributions of committed subject coordinators was that they were able to raise the collective confidence of their school's staff in that subject by interpreting National Curriculum requirements, assisting with planning and providing teachers with advice and activities when they were experimenting with teaching new material. In addition, many teachers were also coping with the new content in the orders by trying 'to read up' in as many unfamiliar areas as possible:

> I mean I haven't done Tudors and Stuarts since I was 10 – I didn't do history. All of us have had a tremendous amount of reading to do. It's teaching yourself first – it isn't the actual teaching, it's the knowledge we lack in certain areas.

However, developing subject knowledge in this way was a slow process. It was even more difficult to keep up with the demands for subject knowledge for supply teachers, those returning to teaching after having a baby or following a period of ill health and those few teachers who had moved from KS1 to KS2. As one teacher put it: 'I'm not greatly familiar with the top end of KS2 yet, as like everything else you are only a few steps ahead of where they [the children] are now and what you are having to deliver'.

Teachers in the sample attended numerous short LEA courses, courses provided by subject associations and 20-day INSET courses in order to try to improve aspects of their subject knowledge. Insights into how far short courses can extend teachers' subject knowledge are provided by a two-year longitudinal study of the development in conceptual understanding of force and energy of 53 primary teachers following an initial short burst of in-service training based upon a constructivist approach (Summers *et al.* 1993). The research demonstrated that well designed INSET can substantially improve primary teachers' understanding of science concepts. However, it also revealed that teachers may retain misconceptions through training and even develop new ones, and there was evidence of 'slipping back' with short term gains no longer being apparent in the long term. Also, there was often a gap between teachers' perceived change in understanding and an objective assessment of this change. Summers *et al.* (1993) conclude that teachers require support following training if they are to reinforce and build on their new learning.

Perhaps not surprisingly there was considerable variation between teachers as to the subjects in which they either felt confident or lacked confidence depending on their qualifications, personal interests and experience. However, certain trends could be identified. The majority of teachers felt competent to teach English and mathematics because these had always had an important place in the primary curriculum. The 1989 and 1991 surveys of primary teachers' feelings of competence in National Curriculum subjects (Bennett *et al.* 1992), carried out as part of the Leverhulme Primary Project (1989–92), also found that teachers were most confident in English and the subject that they felt the second most confident in was mathematics. In the 1989 survey science was ranked third from bottom but by 1991 sufficient teachers felt competent in science that it was ranked third, although the perceived increase in expertise was most marked in the process elements of science and the biological content. In our research most teachers also reported growing confidence in science as experience was built up through teaching it and, in the case of some coordinators, through attendance at 20-day courses and LEA INSET. One teacher, when asked what she particularly enjoyed about her work, identified 'doing science with the children as they love doing the activities and experiments'. Science was a subject a number of teachers now found satisfying to teach because of its potential to interest and motivate children. Technology was ranked tenth in both of the Leverhulme surveys of teachers' feelings of competence and in our research was the subject which teachers considered caused them the greatest difficulty:

> I don't understand technology to be perfectly honest – I think it is very, very difficult. I find fitting aspects of technology into our work very difficult and I know I speak for my KS2 colleagues . . . The technology, to me, was a whole new kind of concept area that was almost beyond my grasp.

The original orders were thought to be 'an absolute nightmare' as the language was regarded as off-putting and difficult to understand and the concepts and skills were ones that teachers either did not possess or were unable to recognize within their existing practice. It is therefore unsurprising that OFSTED (1995) found standards were often low in this subject. While the separate revised order for design and technology supported by SCAA (1995a) guidance is a step towards improving practice through the clarification of requirements, access to high quality in-service training and improved resourcing are much needed.

Textbooks and commercial packages are one means to help teachers to overcome lack of subject knowledge. For some teachers finding the information that they needed to prepare and to resource geography and history was proving especially difficult:

> It would be so much easier if you just had a book that you could just actually dig into. In history, the publishers seem to be coming out

with those books now, so you can actually pick up a set of books and work your way through.

Published materials were regarded as both 'timesavers' and a 'safety net' because if they were produced by well known, reputable companies they were likely to cover everything that was necessary. For example, concern over the teaching of music had led to the widespread purchase of the Silver Burdett scheme to assist the classteacher with little expertise in that subject. In Campbell's (1992) discussion of possible ways forward to cope with National Curriculum overload, he acknowledges that one option would be 'to introduce standard texts or schemes in all, or most, subjects, in which the intellectual content would be provided for teachers, together with examples of learning and assessment tasks in differentiated levels' (p. 14). As, increasingly, specialist advice on the selection of such materials is likely to be unavailable, because of the dismantling of LEAs, he considers that 'state approval, rather like a British Standard, of any text or scheme that meets national curriculum criteria, though not state prescription of one official text might be necessary' (p. 14).

Approaches to specialist subject teaching

One headteacher identified as one of the benefits of the National Curriculum that staff had analysed and shared their subject strengths and weaknesses. He also said how increasingly the school was using the subject expertise of parents and members of the local community:

> I was very like a lot of primary teachers, I think, concerned at first about subject specialization, but I'm beginning to have a strong commitment to it now, because when I stood back and looked, we have a lot of specialization in this school already, not only in the sense of teachers' expertise, but also in the sense of using a lot of outside people who are interested in some dimension – a lot of artists in school, musicians, authors coming and sharing books . . . a retired teacher actually locally who does a whole thing on astronomy and brings things into school and sets up a mini-planetarium. We also know a lot of people locally who can give exciting inputs on conservation and related issues like the local rangers.

Other schools also spoke of their increasing use of parents and volunteer helpers to provide specialist knowledge on a one-off or regular basis. We also encountered, in the schools visited, several retired teachers or teachers who had just moved areas who were going into schools to provide additional help. For example, in one small school a teacher, who was paid travelling expenses only, taught music throughout the school and wrote the school's music policy document. In some schools the expertise of NTAs was also being used with groups of children under the supervision of the teacher – for example, in a primary school extra games coaching in Year 5 and Year 6 was provided by a young male NTA.

In many of the schools in the sample informal exchanges of classes took place, enabling teachers to use their expertise with classes other than their own. Such exchanges occurred across all areas of the curriculum but especially to provide assistance in music and PE – if the school did not have a specialist teacher in those subjects – and in science, technology and art which were thought to require knowledge and skills not readily 'swotted up'. In schools where there was more than one class in a year group such arrangements meant that lessons could be repeated, thereby slightly reducing workloads. For example, in a junior school the language coordinator and the mathematics coordinator both taught Year 3 classes and they swapped classes from break to lunchtime four mornings a week and taught their specialisms. Teachers welcomed such exchanges as they enjoyed teaching to their strengths and not having to teach a subject in which they were less confident. Also, they felt that the children enjoyed meeting another teacher.

It is widely assumed that, as one LEA adviser put it, 'the pressure [from the government] for some increase in specialist teaching at KS2 is clearly raising questions of viability about curriculum delivery in the small schools'. Given this, it was particularly interesting to find that, of the nine small schools with less than 100 pupils in our sample, one had already adopted a flexible staffing structure to create specialist teaching in science, art, music and PE at KS2. The school (94 pupils) had two KS2 classes, each with 27 pupils – one mixing Year 3s and Year 4s and the other mixing Year 4s, 5s and 6s. They had found that, whilst incorporating history, geography and science into topics had worked well in KS1, it had been less successful in KS2, especially in relation to science. Their new strategy involved timetabling all the KS2 children for science on the same afternoon and dividing them into three groups shared between the head, the other classteacher and the part time teacher. The head explained:

> We felt that the Y[Year]6 and the Y5 children were not getting a kind of shove in science to give them experience of the higher levels in the National Curriculum. Also, if you were doing science as a topic in your class, to have the three age groups – I just felt we weren't stretching the older children and so we've sorted them out so Jenny's got the Y5s and Y6s, I've got the Y4s and Paul's got the Y3s. And we each do an AT a term [a different one each].

The two KS2 classes also came together for art, music and PE. Again, flexible use of staffing allowed one teacher to take music and the other PE and then swap over, with a third group doing art with the head – thus enabling each of them to teach to their specialisms. The head thought that there were other advantages in such an arrangement:

> Because it's a small school you're also conscious of the fact that, at the end of their time here, they're going on to a big high school where they're going to have different teachers for every subject and some of the children have only ever had me for everything. And although they see other people – although not very many of them – we thought it was also quite a good idea to give them the experience of going to another teacher for a lesson.

However, she added that it would be very difficult to do this for other subjects as well because of lack of time and the need to preserve an overall curriculum balance. Other difficulties posed by their strategy included the greater attention that needed to be given to record keeping (because they were teaching pupils from someone else's class) and the overlapping caused by some topic teaching containing the same material as parts of the separate subject teaching.

Another small school in our sample, with just one KS1 and one KS2 class, planned to introduce specialist teaching for maths and science in the following year. This was prompted by the headteacher (the KS1 teacher) who wanted to teach maths throughout the school for two reasons: first, 'because I'd like to teach the juniors' and, second, because 'it would be nice to see this progression – working with children right through the school from infants right the way and just follow something through'. She had been on one of the 20-day maths courses and the other teacher in the school was going to take responsibility for science, thus enabling a swap of maths and science teaching across the two classes. Their LEA general adviser was keen to support this and had therefore given the other teacher extra time in which to visit other schools to see science teaching. They recognized, however, that such an arrangement would require very careful planning because of the role that science currently played in the school's topic work.

The classteacher system generally continued to be viewed as important for providing pupils with security and continuity. One headteacher offered two additional reasons as to why there was so little specialist teaching in primary schools:

> I think that people don't want to come out of their own classroom because they think they're going to lose control and track of their own class. Also, I think it's perhaps the feeling that you won't do it well enough and you don't want to put that specialism on show for other people because you are not confident enough.

However objections to subject specialist teaching raised by teachers most frequently related to organizational concerns. For example, there was a feeling that specialist teaching would make it difficult to ensure that pupils completed work and that moving pupils or teachers plus resources between classrooms might prove timewasting or disruptive. Also, staffing levels and structures could not cope with the knock-on effect caused by providing variation in the length of time needed for certain kinds of lessons and for children of different ages.

In the first phase of the research, even in the large schools, the formal timetabling of specialists across the school was unusual, with the exception of music and to a lesser extent PE. However, by the second phase, there was a move towards more planned exchanges for the oldest children. Only two schools in the sample – a primary school (158 pupils) and a 9–13 middle school (225 pupils) – had devised a system in response to the requirements of the National Curriculum whereby more than half of the National Curriculum subjects were taught separately by subject specialists in KS2. The unusual nature of this primary school's willingness to explore the possibilities of specialist teaching makes the model that they have devised extremely interesting. We therefore present here a brief case study which examines the model and presents the school staff's perceptions of its strengths and weaknesses.

A case study: specialist teaching at KS2

The primary school had implemented considerable changes in curriculum organization in order to try 'to get rid of this terrible mire of muddle which is what we seem to have had for the last two or three years as each new thing has come onto the horizon and we have had to take it on board.' The staff were seeking to manage the curriculum more effectively through the use of specialist teaching. The headteacher described how, like many other primary schools, for the past three years the school had developed 'a thematic approach' to teaching the National Curriculum. The themes were largely science-led but included most other curriculum subjects. However, as more of the orders were introduced and the amount to be covered in KS2 grew, the staff became increasingly concerned as to whether this approach was providing a balance in terms of time spent on subjects, adequately addressing all the ATs, achieving progression within subjects and avoiding 'unseen overlap'.

The head explained that to her 'it has always seemed so terribly difficult to plan in themes to actually make sure you are addressing all the areas of the curriculum and giving sufficient weight to each one'. The deputy head had gone on a course on curriculum planning about two years previously and she had come back with a great deal of material on models of planning which the staff considered and from which they took some ideas. However, they remained dissatisfied with their approach to curriculum organization and thought that their planning 'was insufficiently tight and rigorous'. Therefore, the head decided 'let's sweep all of that away and go for broke and try something completely new, which I had actually had at the back of my mind for quite a long time, and see how it works'. In terms of staff subject expertise the school was well placed to move towards specialist teaching because, in acknowledgement of the growing importance of curriculum coordinators, during the six years that she had been at the school she had appointed staff with different curricular strengths: 'Each time an appointment has come up I've looked for the gap and tried to fill it.'

The decision was made to 'isolate' the KS1 staff as they were going to continue to work within a thematic approach:

> We thought this was more appropriate for KS1 because we must give more time to the basic skills and the demands of the National Curriculum at that stage can be met through umbrella themes – so they carried on with that although they needed to dovetail their planning into KS2.

Working on the assumption that all primary teachers could, or certainly should, be able to teach numeracy and literacy, it was decided that each of the four KS2 teachers would teach mathematics, English, RE and some PE to their own class in the morning. As the school was a Roman Catholic primary, more importance to the planning and teaching of RE was found than in the non-denominational primary schools. For four afternoons from Monday to Thursday KS2 teachers would teach their specialist subjects – science, history, geography and technology – to each of the KS2 classes in turn. On Friday afternoons, each class would study either music, art, PE or drama for a period of nine weeks, so that over the year all KS2 pupils would have experienced in-depth teaching in the four subjects. Elements of all of these might also be included in the other subjects. This involved subject specialists taking on another specialism: 'The scientist is the musician, the historian is the artist, the geographer is the PE person and the technologist is the drama teacher'.

The head and the staff developed planning sheets to support the new system; these sheets had been through several revisions and were in use throughout KS2. Teachers did not view the move towards more specialist teaching as bringing about changes to their teaching methods as they claimed to use whole class teaching, various kinds of group and individual work, depending on the nature and purpose of the lesson and available resources. The mathematics lesson observed in the morning with the Year 6 class involved children learning about decimals. They were working individually on the addition and subtraction of decimals from Nuffield Mathematics and in pairs and cooperative groups on games involving the use of calculators. The teacher sat with each pair or group in turn going over the work that they had done and helping them to address aspects they were finding difficult. In the science lesson for Year 4 pupils observed in the afternoon and described in Chapter 2 they were divided into four activity groups. After an initial input by the teacher to go over homework and explain the tasks for each group, the children worked individually monitored by the teacher.

The head said that, after having gone through a term getting accustomed to the new system and developing their planning, staff were now in the process of carrying out an initial review 'to get some feedback on how the system is working'. This was largely to be accomplished by devising a questionnaire for teachers to complete. However, staff had already identified several advantages of the new way of working. Teachers only had the orders for five subjects with which to become familiar, which cut down on work. Depending on the structure of the subject in some instances the amount of planning was reduced. For example, the science specialist taught the same aspect of science across the whole school and modified her teaching to take account of the differing ages and aptitudes of the pupils. Thus in the spring term each class was working on 'The Earth in Space'. The history specialist, who was teaching different study units to each class in order to keep those on British history in chronological order, was not able to reduce planning time. It was thought to be easier to retain the integrity of subjects and ensure that children developed subject-specific as well as generalist skills. The science specialist described how:

> the children are much more aware of those things which make science science. We do a session each morning to record what they have worked on as part of their RoA and we do a diary at the end of the week which sums up their work. Whereas last year however careful you were, they were in considerable doubt about what a particular activities focus was they are very very clear now and they can see where they are going.

Teachers also considered it beneficial to teach their specialist subjects to children of all ages and abilities across the key stage as this enabled them to examine the nature of progression within subjects. The children moved around the school to the specialist teachers which meant that they could make their classrooms specialist areas and so store and use resources more effectively. Work from each class was displayed in the specialist teachers' rooms which meant that children could see what others were doing in each subject throughout the school. Most of the children were thought to enjoy the stimulus of meeting different teachers and working in various parts of the school and apparently feedback from parents suggested that children viewed it as 'grown-up' and 'proper school'. Assessment of individual progress was thought to be made easier in so far as teachers had more clearly defined subject-specific learning objectives for their lessons and had less SoAs with which to become familiar. Records were completed very carefully because they had to be comprehensible to other teachers. Finally, a major advantage identified was that because the KS2 children were being taught by four teachers:

> we discuss them much more – if problems arise or if some really good ideas come from a child or anything that surprised us then we will talk about it in the staffroom and I think that feeds back to the children in a positive way. Also, we make group decisions about what strategies to use with a child who is underachieving.

The benefit of sharing children's successes and difficulties was viewed as outweighing any concerns about reduced interaction with classteachers. Also, as the staff pointed out, the children spent the morning with their classteachers, rounded off the day by spending the last half an hour in the afternoon with them and apart from this time would meet them for specialist teaching one afternoon a week and sometimes again on Friday.

Although staff felt very positive about the new system, it was viewed as having some limitations. First, although 'good use was made of the time available', one afternoon a week was regarded as inadequate because 'there is just too much to cover and you cannot do justice to everything'. While perhaps this problem was more to do with an overloaded National Curriculum than the new system, it was regarded as less flexible than when the children remained with their classteachers and aspects of themes could be allocated varying blocks of time during a day, a week or a half term. There was also a limited amount of time in which all the assessments could be carried out and each specialist needed to have access to the record book of every KS2 pupil in order to record achievement. Subject teaching also exposed the lack of, and generated the need for, resources within subjects when 20 or more children needed to work with similar materials. As the new system was in its first phase, the work that a class did in one subject was totally independent of what was being taught in other lessons. It was intended that when plans were reviewed, the timing of certain subject elements should be adjusted in order to foster cross-curricular links. Finally, although the new system had the whole-hearted support of the staff, they were unhappy with the notion that they might not have opportunities in the future to teach the subjects that they had currently given up. This was due in part to personal interest in some of the other subjects, established expectations that primary teachers should have a range of subject competencies and concerns that it might become difficult to move back into a generalist primary culture to obtain promotion.

Acquiring staff with the range and depth of subject knowledge necessary to teach each of the National Curriculum subjects is an obvious prerequisite for an effective system of subject-specialist teaching. This school, which had four teachers for key stage 2, appears to be the minimum staffing possible to set up a system of specialist teaching which both cuts by half the number of National Curriculum subjects with which a teacher is expected to be familiar and allows a fairly straightforward timetable to be devised which can readily be fitted into a five-day week and easily followed by teachers, pupils and parents. Having one class per year group makes teaching easier by reducing the age range and ability span for which teachers must cater, but the actual exchanging of mixed age classes need cause no additional problems. A timetable for five, six or seven classes at KS2 to participate in an exchange would necessarily be more complex, but it would also open up more possibilities.

National Curriculum planning

Research into the introduction of the National Curriculum (NCC 1990b; Osborn and Black 1994; Pollard *et al.* 1994) reported that teachers were spending a greatly increased amount of time planning and that they were doing so cooperatively in order to ensure National Curriculum coverage across the school and to prevent gaps or repetition in plans. Such cooperative planning represents a significant departure from the individualist culture of primary schools described by Nias (1989) and was consequently a new experience for many primary teachers. While whole school sharing of concerns and ideas was broadly welcomed by teachers, as touched on later in relation to improving continuity and explored more thoroughly in Chapter 7, it was not without tensions and difficulties. Teachers acknowledged that their National Curriculum planning had led them: to plan more rigorously and in greater detail; to look more critically at the learning experiences that they were offering children; and to have clearer objectives for lessons and activities. However, during the fieldwork period attitudes towards planning became less positive. A commonly held view was that there was too much 'planning for planning's sake' and 'we are spending so much time writing down what we are doing we haven't got time to do it'. Much of the paperwork involved in planning was increasingly becoming 'just a burden' which was leading to other aspects of their practice being neglected, such as display and the preparation of lesson materials. Hopefully a major advantage of a moratorium on curriculum change will be that plans can be reused, so saving time in the future.

Schools in the sample were following advice from LEAs to draw up long, medium and short term plans. Initially long term plans consisted mainly of lists of topic titles for the year or key stage. In schools which contained mixed age classes these were frequently on a two-year cycle and, in small schools which had classes with pupils across the whole of KS2, they were usually on a four-year cycle (posing particular problems, which are discussed in Vulliamy and Webb 1995). Medium term plans generally involved topic webs. These either listed the activities to be undertaken, usually under contributing subjects or included more detailed breakdowns of subject areas in terms of the PoS, ATs, resources and school visits. During the period of the fieldwork medium and long term plans tended to become more detailed and included consideration of subjects and aspects of subjects taught separately.

At the end of the first phase of fieldwork, LEA courses and published guidance on curriculum planning, while stressing the need to preserve the integrity of subjects, took a predominantly topic-focused approach and were strongly influenced by development work carried out in KS1. By the second phase of fieldwork, advice was also orientated to KS2 issues and had either been influenced by, or reached similar conclusions to, that provided by the NCC (1993b; updated by SCAA 1995b). The NCC approached curriculum planning through the identification of units of work drawn from a single subject, which fell into two broad categories: continuing units (requiring regular and frequent teaching) and blocked units (discrete areas which can be taught within a specific amount of time). Thus in the guidance provided by one LEA on long term planning, elements of the PoS are grouped into subject building blocks which schools can cut out and place below the line in the planning grid provided if they are ongoing and in the columns if they are to occur for a short time only. This advice appears to have become increasingly adopted by schools across the LEA and was used by one of the small schools in our sample to arrive at their long term plan. It marked a departure from the school's usual planning practice in that planning began from the PoS rather than past topics and activities. Progression was intended to be built in because the blocks were labelled according to the key stage in which they should occur and numbered to show progression of content. However, teachers' prior values and experiences meant that during the planning the identification of possibilities for the integration of the content of blocks and opportunities to take advantage of local and national events led to some blocks being relocated rather than such links being made at the end of the process as advocated by the SCAA (1995b). Although through their planning schools are considering how much time to allocate to aspects of work, there seems little support for the SCAA's (1995b) suggestion that planning should begin with an exact analysis of the teaching time available per week, term and year.

In most schools teachers produced fortnightly or weekly short term plans which were submitted to the headteacher or deputy for information and sometimes for comment. These often contained references to skills and concepts to be taught, descriptions of pupil activities, and in a few cases, strategies for the assessment of learning outcomes and the differentiation of work for pupils of different abilities. Such plans were frequently supplemented by teachers' personal daily plans which took the form of jottings in desk diaries, notebooks or ringbinders about ideas and resources and reminders, such as the use to be made of parent volunteers and specific actions to be taken to meet the needs of individual pupils. An issue raised by a number of teachers was that the short term plans required by the school fulfilled mainly an accountability function and contributed little to the practicalities of lesson preparation.

Planning for the National Curriculum revealed the full complexity of primary education and the demands of primary teaching. Teachers in all the sample schools shared a common understanding that it was actually impossible to teach all of the National Curriculum in its then current form:

> It's impossible to fit everything in. We obviously – probably like others – have come to the reality that we must make our priority the core subjects and work on the English, maths and science to the full extent that they require whilst interweaving some history, geography etc. when we feel that we can do it.
>
> (headteacher, junior school)

Schools' responses to the problem of curriculum overload represented the range of possible approaches to reducing the content of the National Curriculum open to Sir Ron Dearing when he carried out his review: either concentrating on the core subjects or on the 'basics' of numeracy and literacy and adopting a more superficial approach to the rest of the National Curriculum or omitting aspects of all subjects in order to promote the value of the other foundation subjects, especially art and music. Schools were influenced in making these kinds of choices by the perceived needs of their pupils, staff strengths and weaknesses in particular subjects, concerns over SAT results and available resources. At classroom level teachers were also reducing the breadth of the National Curriculum by modifying their original intentions on medium term plans in order to set themselves more realistic goals. Therefore the curriculum as experienced by pupils was likely to fall some way short of original plans and intentions. In addition, as one teacher acknowledged, teachers taking it upon themselves to 'prune' the National Curriculum were reducing continuity between schools and creating potential problems for middle and secondary schools, especially for those who received pupils from a number of first or primary schools as they might not know 'which bits have been trimmed back in various schools'.

While they acknowledged the need both for 'tight' planning and strict adherence to plans in order to ensure coverage, teachers sometimes felt straitjacketed by their plans and unable to take advantage of unanticipated opportunities for learning. 'Having a narrow path to tread down' and 'being document driven' were particularly to be regretted when it meant that there was no time to follow up children's interests. Alexander *et al*. (1992: 20) disagree with such comments stating that: 'too many teachers have argued that rigorous and comprehensive planning militates against the need for spontaneity and flexibility. In fact the two are perfectly compatible'. In the context of an overcrowded National Curriculum teachers in the sample did not experience them as compatible, although some were prepared to set aside their plans in order to maintain spontaneity. One teaching head, who said that once the staff have decided on a plan 'we stick to it', qualified her claim by saying:

> having said that, I would still teach something if a child brought an artefact in, something he was sparked off by, and it was so interesting and I felt that it was so important, I would put everything else on hold and do that.

Teachers also gave examples of plans being set aside to introduce activities based on local events or to take advantage of the expertise of visitors. While it is a matter for schools to decide how far existing plans should be abandoned or postponed in order to take advantage of unforeseen opportunities, teachers need to be clear as to how far and in what ways these are likely to make a superior contribution to pupils' learning than what was planned.

An element of the unexpected and space to diverge from plans is recognized as important in the Schools' Council project, 'Developing children's thinking through topic work' (1981–3). In their account of the project Kerry and Eggleston (1988: 270) conclude that 'certainly the best teachers are those who plan for a variety of outcomes and do not totally pre-condition children's learning, and who think on their feet so as to use the leads and interests of the children'. Mortimore *et al*. (1988: 286) identify as a criterion for school effectiveness the strategy of structured sessions which allow pupils 'freedom to manage their own work within a framework which ensures that important aspects are not omitted, and that time is not wasted'. In his study of critical educational events, Woods (1993: 8) examines in detail the role of 'divergence' and the creative tension between imposed structure and pupil freedom. He values the deliberate building of an opportunity for divergence into events, which he describes as:

> an 'explosion' stage when the children are encouraged to be innovative and creative, explore opportunities, stretch their abilities, experiment with different media and forms of expression to find the optimum ways of working, test and develop their relationships with others. Tight planning within this phase would be counterproductive. There is a strong element of serendipity.

Unforecastable things happen. New, and completely unforeseen, teaching and learning opportunities arise.

Whether balance between subjects should be achieved over a day, a week, a term, a year or a key stage was another issue to be decided on when planning. According to class composition, past practice and preferences, schools came to different decisions. For example, in one junior and infant school half-termly topics had 'a main and subsidiary driver' and balance between subjects was achieved over two years. Linked to decisions on subject balance were considerations of what might be deemed 'a reasonable amount of time' in each subject and how far time allocations were related to the quality of work. For example, it was considered in several schools to be beneficial for pupils to work on technology in large blocks of time for a whole day or several consecutive afternoons in a week in order to maintain pupils' motivation, to enable them to appreciate the relationship between the various stages in designing and making and to make maximum use of the organization required to get the classroom and resources ready.

Many teachers thought that subject balance should be weighted in favour of coverage of the basics of numeracy and literacy. Several teachers felt that the demands of other subjects were 'squeezing English out' and/or causing it to 'be thinly spread' across the curriculum. As one junior teacher explained:

> I've always taught first years [Year 3] and I always used to think that my job was to get the children literate and numerate in the first year and give them a good 'bottoming' so that higher up the school they could actually branch out. But I seem to have so much more to do – geography, history, technology, IT and everything else – that I think the English that we do is getting watered down. I try to bring it into other subjects that I'm doing, whereas in the past, I always made sure that every day I did an English session.

These teachers expressed particular concern that they were giving insufficient time to reading: 'I mean that's one of the things I'm falling down on because of the workload; whereas before I'd hear the children read once a week, now I find it difficult to get round once'. These findings are reflected in the HMI survey of 49 schools (OFSTED 1994b). However, despite the concerns voiced it was considered by OFSTED (1994b: 2) that 'most classteachers strongly protected the time for "basic skills" teaching'. The need to tip the balance in favour of the basics is endorsed strongly by Woodhead (1995: 4), who emphasizes the fundamental nature of literacy and numeracy and claims that at KS2 'unsatisfactory standards in reading and writing are to be found in one in ten and one in four schools respectively' and that 'standards of achievement in number are judged unfavourably in one school in eight'. If through the revision of the orders schools succeed in freeing up the 20 per cent of time suggested, then, given current pressures, this seems likely to be largely devoted to the basics to the detriment of possible alternatives, such as the cross-curricular themes (NCC 1990c), a modern foreign language or a particular area in which the school could develop special expertise.

The planning process confronted teachers with other questions on the relationship between a broad curriculum and a balanced one and how far what might be viewed as a balanced curriculum for the majority of children might prove unbalanced for individuals with particular gifts and needs. Initially discussion of balance centred on the distribution of, and time allocation to, subject content across the curriculum but in some schools this then moved on to a consideration of balance within subjects. Through the planning process alternative interpretations of balance in terms of introducing pupils to skills, concepts and types of activities and tasks arose. The importance of achieving balance in activities was highlighted by Alexander (1992) in his analysis of teaching strategies used during the evaluation of the Leeds PNP project. The Primary Needs Independent Evaluation Project (PRINDEP) team found that 10 'generic activities' underpinned classroom practice regardless of the subject or topic being covered and that these generated different patterns of task-related behaviour:

> Children in our classroom practice sample spent a high proportion of their time working when they were engaged in tasks which involved talking to the class, talking to the teacher, construction, listening or collaboration. Their work levels were lowest in writing, drawing/painting, or tasks which involved movement from one part of the room to another, and all three of these activities generated very high levels of routine behaviour. For the most part, high levels of distraction were found where work levels were low, and the highest distraction levels of all were in tasks involving writing, drawing/painting, and reading.
>
> (p.72)

These findings demonstrate the importance of ensuring that pupils experience a range of alternative activities and teaching strategies during the day and certainly across the week. Also, Alexander (1992: 72) pointed out that 'the striking feature of the activities at which children worked for a high proportion of time was involvement with other people'. This emphasizes the value of planning for pupils to work collaboratively and for classroom assistants and volunteer helpers to provide pupils with opportunities to think aloud about what they are doing through discussion and explaining their work to adults.

The SoAs at each level within the original orders were criticized by teachers: for implying wrongly that each child's learning followed a predetermined order; for at times appearing illogically sequenced or necessitating 'jumps' in understanding; and for being likely to lead to labelling of children by levels. However, the levels of attainment were acknowledged to provide a helpful framework for planning for progression in knowledge, understanding and skills in each subject and for sequencing the activities to be provided. Planning for progression across the curriculum is highly complex because not only do children progress in different ways and at different rates but subjects vary in the emphasis placed on aspects of progression and their relationship to progression in other subjects. The following checklist of what planning for progression might entail has been compiled from the various factors mentioned by teachers when deciding on the nature and the order of work planned for their pupils:

- making links between pupils' existing knowledge and skills and those to be introduced;
- giving pupils opportunities to apply existing knowledge and skills to ever more complex situations;
- setting problems which increasingly require reasoning based on abstract thinking rather than concrete examples;
- moving from working in familiar to unfamiliar contexts;
- moving from an understanding of contemporary situations and events to studying those in the past or speculating about the future;
- moving from the study of local environments to those that are distant;
- proceeding from the study of general characteristics to specific details;
- exploring the relationships between a unique instance and an overarching principle;
- using an ever increasing range of information and information sources;
- enabling pupils to work both independently and cooperatively with increasing confidence and competence;
- developing pupils' abilities to understand assessment criteria and to evaluate their own work.

As can be seen from the above, many aspects of progression involve pupils developing knowledge and skills along a continuum between what are sometimes almost polar opposites. In some cases there is disagreement about which end of the continuum presents the greatest level of difficulty. For example, during the consultation on National Curriculum history there was considerable debate in schools as to whether young children should progress back in time from a study of the most recent past or study history chronologically. Stannard (1995: 6) argues:

> Primary schools need to manage progression because each subject is cut across by the class teacher system. Thus a key principle in primary curriculum management should be the structuring of

progression within subjects across the year groups to counteract the effects of the horizontal organisation. The progression of work needs to be safeguarded at the school (collective level) because it is difficult, and sometimes impossible, to retrieve from an already integrated curriculum, and it cannot be assured by individual action, however gifted the teacher.

Schemes of work for each subject are one way of structuring progression. However, in most primary schools these only tend to exist where they are provided within commercial schemes for mathematics and maybe aspects of English. After the end of the ATL fieldwork, one teacher described how in her school they had decided to draw up schemes of work for each subject as part of a review and rationalization of all their planning and policy documentation. First, the aims and objectives for each subject were stated on an A4 size policy sheet. Second, schemes of work were drawn up, largely drawing on details of subject coverage in existing long and medium term plans and incorporating discussion on progression and points on teaching methods and the use of resources from the original, often quite lengthy, policy documents. Third, as medium term plans were revised and short term plans written, less detail was needed, especially in the former, because they referred to the appropriate parts of the scheme of work.

Some schools in the sample took advantage of particular events or curriculum activities to reach a better understanding of what might be involved in progression. Thus one primary school did a whole school topic on fairgrounds. All the children and teachers working together on the topic meant that it could become a vehicle for staff development in technology and maximum use could be derived from seeking outside support. The children's work, which was mainly models of fairground rides, was displayed in year groups around the hall. This work was analysed to identify the similarities and differences between the work of children of different ages and explanations were sought as to how they might be related to age, ability or the ways in which tasks were set. Another school used the planning and carrying out of a parents' evening workshop on science to examine progression. Preparation for the workshop required them to make decisions about which activities should represent the work of particular classes and during the actual evening teachers were able to observe children of various ages tackling problems and demonstrating equipment. As discussed in Chapter 4, the need to be clearer about what constituted progression in their subject was one of the most common reasons given by coordinators for wishing to have non-contact time in order to work alongside colleagues.

The National Curriculum and the shared planning to which it gave rise was viewed by teachers as improving greatly curriculum continuity between classes, between infant and junior departments and between primary and secondary provision. However, as described by one primary school head, the next stage of getting teachers to open their classroom doors to one another and to share the implementation of their joint plans was proving much more difficult. He explained that in a full inspection earlier in the year the inspectors had pointed out the differences between parallel classes regarding the depth to which the same areas of subjects were being studied and the consequent need for teachers to work together more in order to improve continuity:

> Now it had been my hope that where there were parallel classes those teachers would take the opportunity to say 'Look we've got to do this, let's plan it directly together and do some things at the same time' and so, perhaps, get a cross-fertilization of ideas, a little bit of swapping around of children. I think I was probably being a little bit ambitious to try and link staff that way – you know straight in.

Encouraging staff to find ways of cooperating over aspects of classroom practice appears difficult in such contexts where teachers continue to value classroom privacy; there is little or no non-contact time for them to visit or work in colleagues' classrooms and the design of school buildings negates team teaching.

Apart from depth of subject coverage, other aspects of continuity affecting pupils' experience of the curriculum which can usefully be reviewed are:

- the degree to which pupils are encouraged to be independent;
- pupil participation in decision making;
- the use of pupil self-assessment;
- the range of teaching methods and resources used;
- the criteria and standards employed for the presentation and content of work; and
- the expectations and approaches to assessment.

However, achieving greater continuity of classroom practice is dependent upon teachers sharing their beliefs and practices and being prepared to reach an agreement as a whole school on the approaches that everyone will adopt. In turn arriving at such whole school approaches is dependent upon factors such as the degree of congruence between teachers' personal educational philosophies, school traditions and the management style of the head. Depending on the school culture and the individuals concerned, continuity can be viewed negatively as imposing conformity and stifling teacher creativity or positively as creating a stable environment for learning within which there are a uniform set of expectations and standards to guide the work of both teachers and pupils.

Having developed long and medium term plans for the National

Curriculum in their own schools, heads and teachers spoke of how they were increasingly cooperating with infant, first, middle and secondary schools to ensure that plans dovetailed and to avoid repetition. A deputy headteacher at a junior school described how he had been made aware of the importance of cross-phase planning:

> At a science course I was on we had to ask kids to make a light bulb light up. I tried this with a small group of Y[Year]4 and Y3 children. The Y4s were clueless – all the classic misunderstandings were coming out that I was supposed to take back to the course. When I talked to the Y3s it was 'Oh, we did that last year, it goes something like this', and within two or three minutes they had done it. They'd experienced this in the infants already and I didn't know and that was one of the things that made us sit up and take notice and work together with the infant school.

He also described how the cluster of schools sending children to the same comprehensive had recently agreed on the need for subject coordinators to meet to share problems, plan together and ensure that children received comparable teaching experiences prior to secondary transfer. Primary headteachers also described a range of ways in which they were trying to improve curriculum continuity between themselves and the secondary schools to which they sent their pupils. For example, one head described the setting up of a curriculum continuity group within the pyramid which had drawn up a three-year continuity plan leading to initiatives such as a humanities INSET day and a link project whereby Year 6 children began a piece of work in the primary school and continued it with their secondary teachers after transfer. The moratorium on changes to the National Curriculum promises to provide a context which could further encourage and facilitate such initiatives. If schools are able to stabilize their own plans, assessment procedures and record keeping, they will be in a stronger position to share these with the schools from which they receive, or to which they send, pupils and to experiment with new ideas to improve the process of transition.

four

The changing role of the curriculum coordinator

Alexander *et al*. (1992: 43) present a model of semi-specialization for primary schools which 'is a combination of consultancy/co-ordination in the advisory sense and specialist teaching, but it is also likely to include some generalist class teaching'. The contribution that subject specialists might make to the primary curriculum has been an increasingly important issue since, in acknowledgement of the increasing demands on classteachers made by the expanding primary curriculum, the Plowden Report (CACE 1967: para 556) proposed that 'teachers expert in the main field of learning should give advice to their colleagues throughout the school'. The report also suggested that the oldest children might be taught by teachers other than their classteachers in order to provide more depth in specific subjects. The Bullock Report (DES 1975) on the teaching of English and the Cockcroft Report (DES 1982b) on the teaching of mathematics further endorsed the need for, and value of, primary school curriculum coordinators – also previously known as posts carrying special responsibilities (DES 1978a) and curriculum postholders (Campbell 1985).

More recently, the introduction of the National Curriculum has both created a pressing need to delegate subject responsibilities to coordinators where possible and presented a formidable challenge to teachers' autonomy. While on the one hand these changes can be viewed as encouraging the development of the coordinator's role, on the other hand the pressures on teachers' non-contact time and need for clerical assistance have increased (Campbell *et al*. 1991), so reducing their scope for action. Government and OFSTED pronouncements have stressed the need for better subject teaching in primary schools (Patten 1993a; OFSTED 1994b) and, at the rhetorical level at least, the role of curriculum coordinators has become a high profile one encompassing a wide range of responsibilities with, for example, OFSTED (1994b: 9) suggesting that it should be renamed 'subject manager' because ' "co-ordinators" is too limited a description'.

In this chapter we consider our findings in relation to primary school curriculum coordinators. We begin by briefly reviewing some lessons from previous research on this theme prior to examining the changing nature of the coordinator's role in relation to planning and policy making, resource management, INSET and opportunities to influence classroom practice. We discuss the continuation of the major constraints on the effective execution of the coordinator's role and conclude by considering those changes required at local and national level to enable coordinators to exert greater influence on school policy and practice.

Lessons from previous research

A milestone in the recognition of the possibilities of curriculum coordinators and the school conditions necessary for them to be effective was the inquiry into the nature of school-based curriculum development carried out from 1980–82 by Campbell (1985). He identified the authority of headteachers in curricular matters, the autonomy of classteachers in their own classrooms and the lack of non-contact time and clerical assistance as major factors constraining the work of coordinators. During the same period Reynolds and Saunders (1987) carried out research into the responses of primary schools in one LEA to their LEA policy documentation and subject guidelines. This enabled them to examine the role of coordinators in bringing about curriculum change. They concluded that coordinator impact on school practice was enhanced by the following:

● frequent informal discussion of planning with colleagues;
● demonstration of teaching strategies ('change by example'), often in the coordinator's own classroom;
● offering curriculum content and materials;
● 'high profile' headteacher support, especially in juggling time allocations or providing resources, and in expressing public approval; and, not least,
● 'grafting' and generally, 'putting oneself about' in a non-interfering way.

(Reynolds and Saunders 1987: 207)

However, like Campbell, they found that

it was striking that curriculum discussion, policy formulation, and action had to be 'fitted into' routine classroom and school

commitments, resulting in long periods of inaction, with short
bursts of activity.

(p.205)

In responding to policy requirements heads and coordinators felt the need
to find ways of accommodating these within existing school values and
practices. This led them 'to negotiate unobtrusively with colleagues over
interpretations of requirements' and to show what was needed indirectly
through 'servicing colleagues' needs' rather than giving advice (Reynolds
and Saunders 1987: 209–10).

More recent studies also point to the relatively limited impact that
primary school subject coordinators can make. Thus, for example,
Kinder and Harland (1991: 209), in their longitudinal case study research
into the role of science coordinators in five primary schools, argue that
'the problems of lack of status, time and opportunity for coordinators to
take on an overt professional development or consultancy role were
repeated in all cases'. Consequently, they suggest that whilst some 'lower
order' INSET outcomes, such as resource provision, were effectively
undertaken by coordinators, 'higher order' outcomes, such as the
provision of new knowledge and skills, were rarely achieved or even
attempted by coordinators. Similarly, drawing from data gathered by
open-ended questionnaires from 17 primary school teachers on INSET
courses and from 78 final year BEd students engaged on a curriculum
coordinator training programme in 1992, Edwards (1993: 55–6) suggests
that the role of the curriculum coordinator is viewed in a very limiting
manner: 'the function was seen in terms of the promotion of the subject,
but the developmental, pedagogic aspect of the role in their work with
colleagues was not being exploited'.

Some of the difficulties experienced by curriculum coordinators are
echoed also in the literature on the impact of advisory teachers on
classroom practice in primary schools. While research indicates that
advisory teachers may work in very different ways (see, for example,
Harland 1990), a common finding is the need for broad skills of people
management which go far beyond advisory teachers' subject expertise or
even their role as exemplary classteachers. Thus, for example, in a case
study evaluation of the work of a team of language advisory teachers,
Webb (1989: 49) concludes that 'the advisory teacher's "process" skills
were of equal if not greater importance than her subject knowledge'.
Similarly, O'Mahony and Sollars (1991: 37) lament the fact that 'less than
10% of the advisory teachers appointed under the ESG scheme for
primary science, received any training in interpersonal skills, adult
learning or the processes of change', whilst Alexander (1992) reports that
in the Leeds Primary Needs Programme coordinators appointed to the
schools complained of their lack of prior training in wider leadership

roles. Although there are important differences in the roles of curriculum coordinators and advisory teachers, arising from the fact that the former are working as insiders with their colleagues whilst the latter are brought in to help from outside the school, each group is aiming to improve the quality of teaching and learning in a particular subject or area throughout a school. As the numbers of advisory teachers are rapidly declining (Dean 1994), this puts a greater premium on coordinators fulfilling this function.

Following this brief review of issues concerning curriculum coordinators arising from past research, we review some of the findings of our research into the impact that recent legislative changes are having on their role.

Planning and policy making

Since the beginning of the first phase of fieldwork in October 1992, the accountability of coordinators for the teaching and learning within their subject has been made increasingly explicit through a range of managerial initiatives resulting from parallel innovations. First, the introduction of appraisal has led increasingly to coordinators having written job descriptions which they have negotiated with headteachers. Second, the growth of more systematic and detailed school development plans has led to in-service training for coordinators and their activities being tied to the achievement of specific targets. Third, and probably the most influential, the criteria for use in OFSTED inspections in relation to the teaching and learning of subjects and the duties of coordinators have increased greatly their awareness of, and their anxiety about, the nature and intended outcomes of coordination tasks.

The first important task for coordinators in relation to the introduction of the National Curriculum is to follow the progress of the order for their subject from the working party's interim report to the final order and to become familiar with and to disseminate that Order's contents to staff:

> One of the things I've already done is take a look at the National Curriculum and try and compress it into a nutshell for people who aren't art specialists. As you'll appreciate having all those document folders to look through, it's very difficult for everyone to look through everything – so what I've done, I've compressed the main aims on to one sheet for staff with some guidance as to what they should be pursuing.
>
> (primary school art coordinator)

The next stage is to assist with the development of long and medium term plans for teaching their subject throughout the school in order to ensure that National Curriculum requirements are covered and that there are no gaps or repetition. In some cases coordinators worked with individual classteachers or members of a year group at the planning stage to suggest specific subject activities or assessment tasks. Frequently, as was observed by the researchers, during breaks and lunchtimes coordinators passed on ideas, pictures and books that they came across which they thought would aid the work of particular teachers.

Responsibility for revising or producing policy documents was an important aspect of the coordinator's role, especially in relation to preparing their school for an OFSTED inspection. In some schools coordinators wrote policies themselves in close consultation with the head and/or senior management team. More frequently, the whole school was involved in policy making, at least in the initial stages, and often working parties led by coordinators were set up with document production as the intended outcome. An important part of this process was staff meetings to brainstorm for ideas, to gain feedback on draft documents and to discuss their implementation. As found by Webb (1989), prior to the introduction of the National Curriculum teachers were unaccustomed to organizing and chairing such meetings which were usually the preserve of the headteacher. Although generally anxious and self-conscious initially, coordinators were becoming much more accustomed to, and confident about, leading meetings. The following aspects of organizing and making maximum use of meetings were found through experience to be important:

● consideration of the likely effect on colleagues of the timing, duration and venue;
● the preparation of an agenda in consultation with colleagues;
● documentation to inform the meeting which is circulated in advance;
● the taking of minutes, especially notes of points for action;
● keeping to the intended focus of the meeting;
● ways of arriving at shared perceptions and/or agreements on ways forward;
● deciding when it would be appropriate to include non-teaching assistants (NTAs), supply teachers, governors, parents.

Resource management

In their study of 50 London primary schools where there were 279 teachers holding posts of responsibility Mortimore *et al.* (1988: 70) found that headteachers cited two responsibilities as most commonly carried out by coordinators:

First, that postholders should be responsible for maintaining and/or ordering resources, books, materials etc. Second, that postholders should be able, and prepared, to advise colleagues.

The majority of coordinators in our sample regarded managing resources as a major part of their role. This involved carrying out a resource audit, updating equipment and materials and storing them in such a way as to ensure their maximum use:

> I asked everyone to open their cupboards and we put everything in the hall that was anything to do with maths so I could see what we'd got. I persuaded everybody that we needed to centrally resource certain things and although some resources could be in classrooms we should be able to go into each other's rooms and borrow things and make full use of what we'd got . . . We've taken a year out from buying any published schemes, partly because I think the way forward is to dip into a number of schemes rather than slavishly follow one, and partly because the school was badly resourced for maths materials and we spent our entire allocation, or I have, this year on just updating the maths equipment . . . We've a new area for the maths equipment and I've acquired a trolley and trays and I'm trying to label where everything is.
>
> (junior school mathematics coordinator)

Heads differed on the delegation of subject budgets for the purchase of resources. Some thought it demonstrated trust in their coordinators' expertise, 'gives them some sort of control and ownership' and enabled them to make realistic decisions about what the school should invest in. Other heads felt such delegation could lead to duplication of similar materials across subjects and preferred to coordinate ordering themselves.

Coordinators viewed resource management as a relatively straight-forward task which could be done alone, was non-threatening, and was appreciated by staff for its practical value. Interestingly, J.L. Moore (1992), who analysed questionnaire responses from 222 primary heads (a return rate of 44 per cent) on the role of the science coordinator, found considerable imbalance between identifying the need for, and obtaining, resources and assisting colleagues in their use. We found similar problems where, as one IT coordinator put it, getting staff to use the resources purchased was 'a massive task in itself' and this relates to the increasing responsibilities being given to coordinators for school-based INSET provision.

INSET provision

In most of the schools in the study subject coordinators had been on a range of courses on their subjects varying in length from one-off 'twilight' sessions to attendance at the DES 20-day courses in mathematics and science. Especially in relation to LEA courses supporting the publication of new orders, coordinators fed information back to staff in staff meetings and on training days. However, the extent of the requirements in each subject and the speed at which they were introduced meant that coordinators felt that colleagues were 'bogged down with information' and therefore unable to reflect on the implications of the changes for their practice:

> From a coordinator's point of view you talk about the actual ideas that lie behind the documents and what they entail and it's trying to actually bring this home to teachers and influence what goes on in the classroom. There's so much for them to absorb and it's too much to expect them to take on board, all the ins and outs of a particular subject.
>
> (junior school humanities coordinator)

This view was echoed in the findings of a project on managing the whole curriculum 5–16 (Weston 1994), which involved 461 primary schools and was carried out from 1989–91. Information overload was regarded by senior managers as the main factor constraining whole school curriculum management in primary schools (92 per cent), followed by lack of non-contact time (80 per cent) and innovation fatigue (78 per cent). Some coordinators in our sample also complained that there was often insufficient time for them to disseminate fully course information that they had acquired as only those whose subjects were in the process of being reviewed and developed could have prime time on training days. A few coordinators found that by the time they were given the chance to report back they had forgotten much of what they had been told. Others described how too much had been crammed into training days with the result that by the final session in the afternoon teachers were too tired to absorb anything further.

Especially during the first stage of fieldwork, when training days or parts of training days were devoted to subject areas, time was often geared to getting planning and policy documentation into place. Only occasionally did coordinators lead workshops or discussion sessions where professional development rather than task completion might be viewed as the main orientation. However, increasingly as coordinators themselves and their colleagues thought that they had the appropriate subject expertise, confidence and skills to make inputs, lead discussions and organize workshops, coordinators were both organizing and delivering INSET. For example, in one primary school (270 pupils) the technology coordinator provided a couple of workshop sessions 'where staff have been helped with the basic skills of sawing and cutting, using general tools, fixing things together, so then they can pass that on, hopefully, to the children'. After this, she provided further support in the form of a central collection of books and resources to provide ideas and by displaying the models made by children in her own class for both teachers and children to see.

Coordinators with 'multiple hats' often organized INSET in more than one subject area as explained by a junior school teacher who coordinated IT and mathematics:

> At the moment I'm doing IT INSET which is easy. We have got three Archimedes [computers] and I'm taking three members of staff once a week after school and going through the various disks we've got with them as I feel that's the only way to do it. It's hands on . . . In relation to maths, the end of last term I suppose it was like a reawakening. I took a couple of videos that I'd kept from the OU work [she had completed an advanced diploma with the Open University] and I went into the Teachers' Centre and brought into school all the new and exciting stuff and I did a four week input. I looked at the ATs in turn, very broadly, so that the staff would get a refresher – what was meant by them and what kinds of materials were available which I think went down very well.

As listed below, the activities which coordinators could use as the basis for INSET both after school and during staff development days were many and varied:

- following the advice in commercially produced INSET packs and training videos;
- analysing children's work to identify aspects of quality or the development of skills and concepts;
- listening to a teacher from the school, cluster or a support network presenting ideas and experiences;
- explaining the use of new resources and their implications for practice;
- visiting teachers' classrooms to consider alternative approaches to classroom management;
- watching a video of aspects of classroom practice across the school;
- discussing successful teaching strategies developed through working alongside colleagues or identified through monitoring;
- sharing findings of paired observation;
- attending workshops run by LEA advisers or private consultants;
- visiting a school using the resources or equipment that was going to be adopted;
- whole school attendance at an exhibition or conference.

Teachers found curriculum workshops, which were set up to demonstrate to parents the kinds of work in particular subjects that their children were doing, also served as an update for colleagues on possible ways to use new resources and equipment as well as providing a valuable and enjoyable learning experience for children and contributing to positive relationships between teachers and pupils. As one primary school science coordinator explained:

> All that [parents' evenings] is extra to the curriculum and yet it isn't, it's part and parcel of it. The science evening for parents and children with hands-on activities, my children set that up and it was a very valuable activity for them. Although I did the cards and things, I gave groups of children the cards and they had to collect the equipment for their experiment, set it out in the hall and then they were asked if they could monitor it through the evening – be around to keep it tidy, make sure that bits didn't go missing, that they were there to explain to people how it worked. Because they had set it up themselves they really felt they owned it. They were marvellous, and as it came fairly early on in the year it made a bond between us much more than if we hadn't done something like that.

In order to provide INSET which is valued by staff, coordinators considered that a necessary prerequisite was to understand their needs and to identify issues to be addressed arising from current practice. However, although the impetus of externally imposed reform may have had the unintended consequence of promoting and strengthening co-operation in schools, as documented by Nias *et al.* (1989) the development of trusting relationships can be a slow process. Consequently, in schools, which had yet to develop such staff relationships, coordinators were uncertain how colleagues were coping and what their INSET needs might be:

> I don't feel, I have to confess, that I know exactly enough about what the staff are finding difficulty with. I find generally the staff are reluctant to discuss their problems, if you like, in case it looks as if they can't cope. I feel that I do it myself, as you really don't want to lose face, and at the moment we are still working on establishing a climate where people can admit that they are having difficulties in an area.
>
> (junior school mathematics coordinator)

Coordinators tended to evaluate the success or otherwise of the INSET they provided according to their perceptions of teachers' reactions at the time, whether they asked for further advice and if the uptake of ideas could be seen in pupils' work. However, a few schools had reviewed the format of school-based INSET in staff meetings and/or introduced questionnaires for completion after sessions in order to gain feedback.

Influencing classroom practice

In the sample schools coordinators helped colleagues to improve their teaching of that subject mainly through answering their questions, discussing with them their practice and children's work and supplying them with ideas for activities and resources. J.L. Moore (1992) also found that science coordinators helped colleagues predominantly through talking, explaining and answering questions rather than classroom-based activities, but suggests that this was not only linked to coordinator lack of non-contact time but also to the belief held by many headteachers that coordinators should not make decisions affecting the classroom actions of colleagues. Similarly, in their study of the role of science coordinators, Kinder and Harland (1991: 198) found that they were not expected to have a direct influence on classroom practice:

> The role, even when undertaken with the utmost efficiency and commitment, was essentially one of servicing that practice and, in a more general sense, promoting the subject area amidst the school's other curriculum demands.

They found that headteachers regarded coordinators as a 'support package' which teachers could choose whether or not to draw on at their own discretion. However, the findings of the OFSTED (1994b) survey, which focuses on primary matters related to the quality of teaching, makes it clear that coordinators are expected to have a central role in curriculum development. Also, in preparation for OFSTED inspections, headteachers were encouraging coordinators to become familiar with those sections of *The Handbook for the Inspection of Schools* (OFSTED 1993b) relevant to their coordinating role. Adopting the advice of coordinators, if legitimated by the handbook, is no longer likely to be regarded as optional as found by Kinder and Harland (1991).

In common with other writers, Bennett *et al.* (1994: 35) have advocated that a useful strategy would be for 'teachers with subject specialisms to work alongside colleagues'. Many coordinators in our sample, who had not experienced working alongside colleagues, wanted to do so not only to support colleagues but also for their own professional development. The wish to develop a better understanding of the nature of progression within their subject, to experience working with children who were older or younger than those that they generally taught, was expressed frequently. Being known to be experienced in, or capable of, teaching throughout the school was an important factor in determining a coordinator's credibility and authority. Infant teachers were thought to be particularly sceptical, and rightly so, of advice offered by coordinators who 'know nothing about infants'. Also, whole school planning becomes a more feasible reality when all involved appreciate the aptitudes and demands of age groups across the school.

In only a few schools was supporting teachers in their classrooms a regular planned and timetabled activity. For example in a 9–13 middle school a deputy head, who was also the coordinator for history and geography, explained that a curriculum area within a year group was highlighted for development each term. Coordinators would then work with teachers in their classrooms to try to improve the quality of learning taking place by looking particularly at what children were doing, how the work was differentiated, the appropriateness of worksheets and printed materials and the use of other resources. He considered that working alongside teachers was vital if changes in practice were to be made:

> I work to my strengths when I'm giving support. I've found from experience that you have meetings with people and it's a hit and miss affair. Actually getting people going in to see whether what you have just talked about is actually working and doing some work towards it, rather than just telling people how it should be done, that seems a much better way forward.

At the time of the interview he was working with the Year 6 teachers to improve the history and geography component of their topic on transport.

Coordinators working with classteachers in the way described above have the potential to extend their range of appropriate approaches to teaching the different facets of subjects, especially if such coordinator support occurs within a programme of school-based INSET. However, as discussed later in this chapter, not only does lack of non-contact time militate against such collaborative activities, but so also do interpersonal factors, such as differences in status and authority and feelings of insecurity on behalf of the coordinator.

OFSTED (1994b: 6) found that in the 49 schools visited very few coordinators 'had a role which extended to monitoring or evaluating the quality of work in their subjects'. In our sample schools monitoring National Curriculum coverage, the implementation of short term plans and the realization of policies in practice was done largely in an informal and opportunistic way through scrutinizing teachers' plans, examining displays and discussing pupils' work and teacher assessments. Visiting classrooms to observe for monitoring purposes seldom occurred, owing to lack of both non-contact time and skills in monitoring. However, in a primary school (which is participating in our current comparative research project on the management of curriculum change in England and Finland), as a result of their recent OFSTED inspection coordinators in the core subjects have been given an hour each week to monitor their subjects throughout the school. While on the one hand this has given them valuable insights into the teaching of their subject, on the other hand it has posed problems which they had not anticipated. These are concerned with what to do with the evidence gathered, when and whether the head should be kept informed of findings and how to raise with colleagues those aspects of their practice considered unsatisfactory. The experience of these coordinators demonstrates the need – well in advance of going into classrooms – to negotiate with colleagues the purpose, process and outcomes of such monitoring and to decide on the focus of classroom observations, how these observations will be recorded and who will have access to them.

Whitaker (1993: 125) values feedback on practice, such as that which could be provided by coordinators in a monitoring role, for its 'enormous potential for improving skills, qualities and performance'. However, he recognizes that it needs to be given with great sensitivity to 'the background and experiences that have made people the way they are and determine their patterns of behaviour' (p. 125). In offering feedback he stresses the need to be non-judgemental and suggests that there are four key factors of which to take account:

1 Be specific and concrete – concentrate only on what has been seen and heard and avoid making inferences and assumptions.
2 Be brief – limit feedback to a few key observations and allow the recipient to respond.
3 Be descriptive – provide only factual accounts of behaviour observed.
4 Be reflective – listen fully to responses, encourage critical reflection and identify ways of improving.

As he comments, if feedback is handled badly it is more likely to close down opportunities for discussion than to stimulate reflection and subsequent change. If teachers are not adequately prepared when first introduced, professional critique can all too readily be taken as personal criticism, which can be damaging for staff relationships. Schools that are building monitoring responsibilities involving classroom observations into the role of coordinators should wait to begin observing until all staff understand fully what is involved and coordinators are clear and feel confident about what is expected of them.

Continuing constraints on the coordinator's role

There are three contextual factors which continue to constrain curriculum coordinators in their role. These are: first, coordinator expertise; second, lack of time for coordination tasks; and, third, the nature of power relationships within the primary school. We will discuss each of these briefly.

Coordinators having responsibility for curriculum areas in which they have the least qualifications and experience are a longstanding source of jokes and myths in primary schools. The coordinators that we interviewed had acquired the role both because of their relevant subject qualifications and/or experience or through showing an interest in, and a willingness to attend courses in, their subject:

> I did art and design as a minor subject at college but really I've just picked things up through the years on courses. I think coordinators these days in the primary school aren't necessarily specialists. I mean, I started as a PE coordinator, then I was humanities coordinator, then a science coordinator and now I've got technology.
>
> (primary school technology coordinator)

Headteachers were divided over the priority that they gave to qualifications in subjects when they made new appointments. Some had systematically over time pursued a policy of acquiring teachers with expertise in different subjects – as in the case of the primary school portrayed in Chapter 3 which introduced specialist subject teaching in the afternoons for KS2. However, the majority of headteachers were of the opinion that applicants' classteaching credentials were of greater importance than their subject knowledge which, if necessary, could be developed in post. The headteacher of a relatively small primary school expressed this view when she described the appointments that she had made during the last two years:

> The last three appointments I made very open ones because I felt I wanted quality teachers. A quality teacher can cope with most things and if they can't they find a way of doing so. If you go for a specialist teacher you narrow the field of applicants down and you could put quality people off applying. The last appointment was made out of a field of about 200 and as a result I have three very good young teachers.

In small schools subject responsibilities had to be shared amongst very few teachers, irrespective of their subject knowledge. In some cases the burden of producing policy and planning documents fell almost entirely on the headteachers who, as teaching heads, had to do the work during evenings and weekends. Senior staff in medium size schools receiving allowances were likely to be responsible for two or three subjects and to have additional coordinating responsibilities for areas such as KS1, KS2, assessment, SEN, behavioural support, equal opportunities, health education, home/school liaison, liaison with secondary schools and staff in-service training. Only some teachers were able to receive incentive allowances for their work as coordinators. While C and B allowances were permanent allocations, the A allowances, especially in larger schools, tended to be temporary and awarded for periods of between one term and two years on a competitive basis (in September 1993 a new 18-point pay spine superseded the old allowance structure, but reference to the old allowances continued in our data from many schools). As the headteacher of a primary school (254 pupils) explained:

> The two As are awarded for a curriculum initiative; in the usual case it's for somebody to revamp the existing policy, organize staff meetings and working groups, and look at the resources and bring our policies up to date. They move around every year. In fact I mean at the moment I'm sharing one of the As for six months. Two teachers have both got it for six months but they've got half each because they're working on the same thing.

While headteachers regarded using A allowances in this way as helpful for getting curriculum initiatives underway, they found that staff commitment to maintaining them tended to dwindle once the allowance was removed.

The second constraint concerns lack of time. Coordinators were also classteachers and as such had experienced an exponential growth in paperwork relating to planning at whole school and classroom level, teacher assessment, recording and reporting to parents. They also had to develop knowledge of the National Curriculum and extend their teaching skills in relation to differentiation and assessing the products and processes of pupil work. Their coordinating responsibilities had to be carried out in parallel with their increasing class commitments. As found in the research by Campbell (1985) and Reynolds and Saunders (1987), coordinators generally had little or no non-contact time. Consequently, many coordinators felt that there was an enormous discrepancy between the rhetoric and the reality of what they were able to achieve:

> Whatever comes out of that [the LEA in-service for coordinators] at the end of the day you are still a teacher with your own class in a school with no time to do what you should be able to do. Whatever I should be doing, there is a difference between that and actually physically being able to do it, that's my problem.
>
> (junior school IT coordinator)

Another coordinator for IT summed up the views of the majority of curriculum coordinators:

> Providing non-contact time is vital, in my opinion, for curriculum development to take place because otherwise the coordinators are stuck in their own room for 100 per cent of the time and the only

time they can get out is after school, which really is not an effective way of really getting the curriculum areas worked on. You need to be able to look at the resources being used. You need to talk to people about x, y and z.

One junior school teacher's weekly allocation of between 15–25 minutes non-contact time during hymn practice and 20 minutes, when her class was being taken for music, was fairly typical. As she put it: 'It's just the case of marking the odd book, or getting something out that you didn't have time for before as you can't get to grips with anything seriously in that time'. She carried out her work as IT coordinator after school. Perhaps the benefits of very small amounts of non-contact time are in the way they serve to provide a breathing space and so briefly relieve the pressure and stress experienced by many teachers.

Over the duration of the research we found that an increasing concern in many schools to keep down class sizes, for reasons discussed in Chapter 1, was resulting in all teachers being class-based, with a corresponding shift from 'floating' to 'class-based' deputy headteachers (see Chapter 5). This meant that non-contact time could only be provided by supply teachers and non-teaching heads and was consequently becoming less, rather than more, frequent. At the point that their subject was the focus of a whole school review, generally in response to the introduction of the subject order, some extra time was usually created. This was largely provided by the headteacher, in a very few schools by the deputy headteacher or music specialist and occasionally by the use of supply staff. A few schools, especially those where coordinators were allocated non-contact time, had set up whole school or coordinator discussions to clarify the work, purposes and priorities for coordinators and to obtain general agreement about the ways in which non-contact time was to be used. As a result, policies for coordination were drawn up which set out exactly what might be expected of coordinators and how the success of the support that they provided might be evaluated.

Coordinators spoke not only of the problem of needing time to carry out their curriculum responsibilities but also of finding times when other members of staff were available for discussion. The problem of finding opportunities to meet with colleagues is not one that can be much alleviated by the provision of more non-contact time for individuals, since during any non-contact time given to coordinators everyone else was teaching. After school teachers often had work relating to their own coordinating responsibilities to do, extracurricular activities or meetings outside school to attend. At lunchtimes they were generally busy preparing for the afternoon's lessons or assessing or recording work.

The main reason given for coordinators not working alongside colleagues in the classroom was the lack of non-contact time needed for this to happen. However, some coordinators felt that even given the opportunity, initially it might be difficult to instigate as teachers still lacked confidence in, and experience of, sharing their classroom practice with others. This related to the issue of existing power relationships within schools. Some young coordinators were concerned particularly about trying to influence the practice of older and more senior members of staff:

> Personally I find it quite hard sometimes because I'm very aware that a lot of members of staff have got a great deal of expertise and experience, whereas I am very new. I think they can offer a great deal to me. I'm very aware of drawing on them.

Relatively new teachers were also nervous about colleagues watching them teach as they were uncertain, owing to their lack of experience, how good a role model they might be. However, as acknowledged by Day *et al.* (1993: 121):

> working in another classroom inevitably involves observation and perhaps consequent nervousness, but if a teacher 'under obser-vation' today is 'observer' in another classroom tomorrow a collaborative atmosphere should be engendered where all value visiting each other's classrooms and accept its consequences.

If lessons could not be observed, then constructive feedback on actual teaching methods and plans in action could not be offered. In addition, the traditional culture of primary schools, which respects class teacher individuality, privacy and autonomy, combined with the desire to avoid placing a strain on staff relationships in a climate where teachers already feel stressed, discouraged open and frank discussion. While the provision of support in classrooms in order to contribute to the improvement of practice was generally valued, doing so in order to monitor the implementation of policies and plans was considered by some coordina-tors to be the kind of surveillance of colleagues' work that was the responsibility of the head or deputy. As one adviser/inspector explained:

> There is a basic insecurity and coordinators are uncomfortable in other's classrooms. They have a hang up, see it as kind of snooping on a colleague and I think you have to get over that hump first. They are quite comfortable to be released to do things like resources or writing documents but less comfortable with monitoring planning across the whole school. I think that there aren't a lot of heads into facilitating that although it's beginning to happen, as they see it as a way of assisting them as the coordinator can look at issues of progression and continuity across the whole school, but it's only embryonic. It will have to develop to spread the workload as you

cannot expect heads to know across nine subjects whether teachers are into all the necessary intricacies.

As is discussed in Chapter 6, in preparation for OFSTED inspections and as a quality assurance mechanism, headteachers are increasingly monitoring classrooms according to the criteria set out in the OFSTED handbook. Also, a few are beginning to involve coordinators in the process, especially if they are members of the senior management team. As is happening in relation to headteacher time, in the foreseeable future any time that can be made available for coordinators to have access to classrooms may be used for them to develop and carry out a monitoring or even inspectorial function. While such a function is unlikely to be welcomed by coordinators, it is likely to be accepted in the current climate of anxiety in which schools are prepared to do whatever they perceive as necessary in order to avoid the stress and ignominy of being deemed as 'failing'.

Improving coordinator effectiveness

Our research suggests that curriculum coordinators are playing a major role in whole school curriculum planning and policy making and raising the collective confidence of staff in their subjects. Confidence raising is achieved predominantly through interpreting National Curriculum requirements, helping teachers to build these into plans and providing ideas and activities for classroom teaching. Coordinators did not view themselves as making more than minor contributions to their colleagues' conceptual understanding of subjects. Given the research on primary teachers' lack of knowledge of many subjects (Bennett *et al.* 1994), referred to in the previous chapter, for them to have held more ambitious aims in this respect would clearly have been unrealistic. However, they did consider it their responsibility to influence the teaching of their subjects, although as discussed in the previous sections, there were major operational constraints on them doing so. Frequently, the introduction of new resources by the coordinator provided the opportunity to raise pedagogical issues because, if the resources were to be used as the producers envisaged, changes to colleagues' classroom organization and teaching methods were often necessary. However, coordinators' abilities to modify other teachers' pedagogies appear to be largely determined by their colleagues' subject knowledge. First, Alexander (1992) argues that there is an inextricable relationship between the depth of teachers' subject knowledge and the range of general teaching techniques open to them – especially extending pupils' learning through higher order questions and providing critically constructive feedback. Second, while coordinators supplied teachers with practical ideas for demonstrations and activities and examples of the application of subject concepts in real life, teachers' abilities to make full and appropriate use of these seem likely once again to be determined by the extent of their subject knowledge.

If coordinators are to be able to meet the new and ever increasing demands of their role and have more influence as agents of change in relation to practice as well as to policy, then they need opportunities to develop the appropriate process skills. First, as identified by Galton *et al.* (1991: 119–20) 'without some training in informal evaluation techniques, including observation, coordinators will not be sufficiently alerted to areas of classroom practice which need modification'. Training in the techniques of classroom observation and the range of purposes it can serve, including analysing pupils' learning strategies and monitoring subject implementation, appear to be a priority. Second, coordinators need courses and in-school support to develop the skills and interpersonal qualities required for leadership, teambuilding and training adults. Third, they require an understanding of the processes of bringing about curriculum change and the factors which constrain and facilitate such change. Fourth, if the provision of INSET is to become a recognized part of the work of primary teachers, then coordinators need further training in the analysis of INSET needs, ways of meeting those needs and evaluating provision so that it can be improved. The coordinators who appeared the most confident in providing INSET tended to be those who had previously participated in LEA INSET provision – an informed source of training which is rapidly disappearing.

Coordinator INSET in these areas is likely to be piecemeal and experienced largely through short courses and one-off training sessions. In order to bring the various elements into relationship with one another and be able to apply them in their schools, coordinators need support after training has been completed. This point has also been made in relation to training in subject knowledge (Summers and Kruger 1994). In a context where school INSET budgets are overstretched, a partial solution adopted by some of our sample schools was to set up area coordinator networks for specific subjects. Coordinators met on a regular basis, rotating around each other's schools, to share intitiatives and concerns. Periodically their schools jointly funded external subject specialists to provide updates, tackle problematic aspects of subjects or visit them in their schools.

Subject coordination, especially planning and providing INSET, was a source of job satisfaction and professional development for those coordinators who considered that what they provided was appreciated by, and helpful to, staff. However it can be viewed as diverting time and energy from preparation that might have been given to their own classroom teaching. If coordinators are to be both effective classteachers and fulfil their coordinating roles, they must have non-contact time. The introduction of the National Curriculum has greatly increased the planning, classroom preparation and assessment in different subjects carried out by primary teachers as well as generating additional responsibilities for subject coordinators. This has rendered the funding disparity between primary and secondary school staffing an anachronism – a view that has been accepted by the House of Commons Select Committee on Education (1994). While some LEAs have made an attempt to redress the situation, power to reduce the present disparity lies mainly with central government. If it is serious about wishing to raise the quality of subject teaching in primary schools, more non-contact time will need to be made available to curriculum coordinators and this, in turn, will necessitate enhanced funding to increase staffing flexibility.

five

The changing role of the deputy headteacher

While there is a wealth of research and advice on primary headship there appears to be relatively little on the role of the deputy headteacher. The contribution to primary schools made by deputy heads is frequently invisible in the literature on primary school management or only considered in relation to their situation as 'trainee head' (see for example, Waters 1987). They receive occasional discussion by HMI (see for example, DES 1985b). Also, research into primary school effectiveness (Mortimore *et al.* 1988) and change in primary education (Nias *et al.* 1989; Alexander 1992) provide some insights into what deputies' roles may entail. However, there is a pressing need for more information on the experience of being a primary school deputy in order that the role as currently practised can be understood, evaluated and more effectively utilized.

This chapter reports the experiences and perceptions of deputy heads and identifies the ways in which their role has expanded and the particular trends in their work since the ERA. We discuss the main issues raised by deputies: non-contact time; 'floating deputies'; curriculum leadership; relationships with the staff and the head; and taking over the headteacher's role. We conclude by considering the need for deputies to develop new skills to fulfil their increased responsibilities and the ways these might be developed through courses, support networks and school-based training.

An expanding role

Mortimore *et al.* (1988) provide a picture of the role of deputy heads in 50 London schools prior to the ERA. They found that for most deputies –

three-quarters of whom were also classteachers – 'the most important part of their role was connected in some way with the interpersonal relationships between the headteachers, teachers, parents and pupils' (p. 51). The other main aim cited by one-fifth of deputies concerned 'the creation of good standards' and several also emphasized the need to be able 'to take over and fill in for anybody' (p. 51). Data on deputy heads' roles in the initial stages of the introduction of the ERA are provided by a survey of deputy heads carried out towards the end of the evaluation of the Leeds LEA Primary Needs Programme (1986–90). This showed that they undertook very diverse responsibilities, but four activities emerged as particularly prominent:

● class teaching;
● curriculum leadership;
● general managerial responsibilities, delegated by the head;
● staff development and staff pastoral support.

(Alexander 1992: 109–10)

Curriculum leadership was the second most frequent responsibility, probably reflecting the pressures on curriculum review and planning resulting from the implementation of the National Curriculum. Alexander (1992) found that most deputies carried out a school-wide responsibility from the above list in combination with 'more idiosyncratic' responsibilities of which taking assemblies, staff–head liaison and pastoral care – in that order – were the most frequent.

> However, there were some whose role appeared to involve, apart from class teaching and standing-in when the head was absent, no more than relatively low level jobs like reporting on leaking gutters or running a tuck shop.
>
> (Alexander 1992: 110)

All deputies in our sample talked of how their workload had expanded enormously since the implementation of the National Curriculum. First, they experienced this in their role as classteachers with the need to acquire new subject knowledge, the increase in paperwork associated with National Curriculum planning and the demands of National Curriculum assessment and recording. Second, ever increasing demands were made on them in relation to curriculum leadership. This was especially the case in schools where there were insufficient teachers to provide coordinators for all subjects or in the very few schools where coordination was only undertaken by those with allowances, which meant that deputies oversaw a range of subjects.

All the deputies were coordinators of one or more subjects – usually including a core subject – and/or an area such as assessment, special educational needs (SEN) and staff professional development and INSET.

Some also oversaw a phase of the curriculum for a key stage or in a minority of cases had been delegated the role of curriculum leader for the school by the head. While responsibility for staff professional development and INSET was generally undefined and underdeveloped, it is a potentially important and demanding role. All deputies allocated this responsibility ensured that staff were aware of the courses available to them and some kept a record of course attendance. However, increasingly the role is likely to include managing the INSET budget, negotiating with individual members of staff their entitlement within that budget and maintaining a balance between funding INSET to meet the specific needs expressed by individuals and/or identified through the appraisal process and school needs specified in the school development plan. Also, it may be useful for INSET coordinators to compile professional development portfolios to chart staff INSET experience, both school and personally funded, in order for the school to have a full record of staff expertise upon which to draw. In addition, such portfolios could serve as a basis for discussion with colleagues about their needs at different points in their careers and maintaining a balance between short practical courses geared to new initiatives and getting a job done and more long term opportunities for reflection and learning of a deeper nature.

While all deputies had experience of taking assemblies, unlike the deputies participating in Alexander's (1992) research, this was not regarded as a particularly important part of their role. Probably this was partly because classteachers also often took assemblies on a rota basis and partly because headteachers were taking more assemblies themselves in order to provide non-contact time. Most deputies interviewed described themselves as fulfilling some 'nuts and bolts jobs' such as 'running sports day', 'selling sweatshirts', 'putting out the chairs for assembly' and 'arranging residential trips and school visits'. Also, deputies tended to take on extra duties – such as arranging a visit by a speaker or theatre group for classteachers – or doing menial tasks – such as tidying the staffroom. As one deputy headteacher explained: 'People are under a lot of stress because there is always too much to do in the day and I probably take on more myself because many people can't be asked to do any extra really'. The school day for many deputies consisted of 'a frantic round' of unceasing activity with little time 'to grab a cup of coffee or a sandwich'. Headteachers were described by their deputies as having become increasingly preoccupied with the budget, administration and teacher appraisal. Consequently the majority of deputies anticipated that their workload and influence, not only in relation to managing the curriculum but also in other areas of management, was going to continue to grow.

Prior to the introduction of appraisal deputies' roles appear to have been based largely on implicit understandings between them, their headteachers and colleagues. For example, in the PNP evaluation over half of those surveyed did not have job specifications (Alexander 1992). Currently, the requirements of appraisal have meant that increasingly specifications are being written down. However, the lack of non-contact time for work outside the classroom, a concern only to write down that which can realistically be accomplished and a preference to keep roles flexible to respond to new and shifting demands, means that on paper deputies' job descriptions tend to be essentially the same as those for other staff. As one deputy head, describing her role, put it:

> A lot of things that I do just happen – there's no clear sort of definition. I think that Julie sees me as her deputy and so I do all the jobs that she would do at different times, if she is not available, or if it is appropriate for me to do it.

Deputies described how they had developed their roles based on their head's expectations, the role of their predecessors, their own understanding of what the job should entail, and demands arising from the implementation of the ERA. A deputy headteacher of a junior and infant school (270 pupils), who had been in post for about a year, said of her responsibilities:

> I haven't got a job description as such. I just do what I think a deputy head ought to do and that's based on my experience of being here and of working for another deputy head and also when I went on secondment seeing what the deputy head did in other schools. Making visitors welcome, anyone coming into the school, making sure they are looked after. Well if I'm available to do that. If not, making sure that somebody else sees to them – overall, sort of care and tidiness of the school and delegating jobs to people. If I think an area needs tidying up or a display needs changing, finding somebody to do it, and of course being responsible if the head's out of school. If the head's busy, I tend to take on discipline problems at lunchtime.

Class priorities and non-contact time

In our research sample the majority of the deputy headteachers were also full time classteachers. For these deputies relationships with the pupils in their classes, lesson preparation, assessment and record keeping took priority over all other responsibilities. They explained that when they took work home in the evenings and weekends they usually tackled class related work first. Their role as a classteacher was viewed as the central part of their work, which they did not wish to lose, especially because, as headteachers were doing less and less teaching, staff looked to them to exemplify 'good' practice. Consequently, they were concerned that the demands of their other roles were consuming their time and energy, and the increase in interruptions during lessons as a result of these demands was having a detrimental effect on their teaching. They shared the views of the deputy who felt that she could 'influence the curriculum quite a lot by actually having a class and passing on good ideas from what the children have done in my class'. However, she would 'like to have half a day each week to go around and give a bit of input into classrooms to get subjects going that people are struggling with'.

Some deputies in our sample only had non-contact time occasionally when supply cover was brought in to release them for a specific task. Others were given between one lesson and one day a week of non-contact time to carry out their extra duties. Those with little or no non-contact time considered that it was vital if they were to do curriculum development work and to find out more about the strengths and the weaknesses of the teaching throughout the school. However, one to one and a half days was regarded as the maximum non-contact time that a deputy with responsibility for a class could have and still retain the in-depth knowledge of, and relationships with, the children in that class. One deputy of a primary school (237 pupils), who represented a tiny minority of deputy headteachers, thought that ideally because of 'the amount of managerial work that has to be done to help the staff to develop themselves and get through every day, we should be aiming for non-teaching deputies'.

The increasing concern to keep class sizes down meant that there were very few 'floating' deputies. A deputy headteacher of a junior and infant school (252 pupils) who was a 'floating deputy' at the beginning of the fieldwork viewed his main role as assisting the headteacher in the management of the curriculum. This included an overview of planning, particularly in relation to the structure of topic work throughout the school, coordinating the ongoing work being done by coordinators on National Curriculum subjects and assessment and record keeping. He was 'floating' because, although the number of pupils in the school warranted an additional classteacher for the juniors, there was no space available in which he could base a class. Consequently he taught a full timetable from Monday to Thursday providing one lesson a week non-contact time for the four junior teachers, withdrawing groups of pupils with special educational needs, teaching technology – his special- ism – to half classes and team teaching to provide the classteacher with opportunities to work with a small group and to carry out pupil assessments.

Despite an acknowledgement of the benefits and flexibility provided by a deputy working in this way, the feeling throughout the school was that smaller classes would be preferable. Consequently, it was intended that once the mobile classroom arrived he would once again be class-based. This intention was realized and at the time of the second interview he was teaching a Year 3/4 class and had no regular non-contact time. He had valued the opportunities provided by 'floating' for his own professional development and considered that access to classrooms and teachers' concerns had contributed to the school's curriculum development. However, he pointed out that during his first year he had 'felt a bit ill at ease because I didn't have that security of my own class' and, partly because his credibility as a classteacher was not established in the school, he had to work hard to gain the respect of his colleagues. Also, as the practice of working alongside colleagues was fairly unfamiliar, building up a relationship of trust so that teachers felt 'comfortable' with him in their classrooms took time and sensitivity. Overall, he felt that 'floating' had a number of disadvantages:

> If I had been 'floating' for three or perhaps four years, you do lose touch with some of the nitty gritty – what is involved in organizing the National Curriculum in the classroom, what that experience is like. I think also you lose touch with some of the issues which as a deputy you might want to bring out in meetings with the head or in a staff meeting – something comes up and you can speak with some authority on it because you're going through the same thing.

Curriculum leadership

A questionnaire survey to deputy headteachers (Purvis and Dennison 1993: 17) found that deputies made a major contribution to the school curriculum as, of the 31 respondents,

> all bar three reported that their job descriptions involved coordination of a National Curriculum area – 12 for more than one area; with twice as many claiming a major involvement with whole school curriculum development in a management role.

Deputies in our sample also coordinated one or more subjects – for example, the deputy of a primary school (296 pupils) was coordinating history, geography and RE and at the time of the interview he was also responsible for music, but that was going to be taken on by a colleague. Unlike this deputy most had responsibility for a core subject. He was allocated history and geography as they were subjects he had studied when training and 'as far as RE is concerned, I suppose I am one of the few who regularly attends church – I'm not saying that's a qualification but some would argue it is'. It was also the deputy's role to pick up subjects for whom there was no obvious member of staff to whom it could be allocated. The ways in which deputies in the sample carried out their roles as subject coordinators was essentially the same as that of other coordinators discussed in the previous chapter, apart from the fact that as deputies they were perceived as having greater influence over both the head and the staff in the implementation of their subjects.

In a few of the largest schools the headteachers stated that they had fully given the role of curriculum leadership to their deputies. As will be explained in Chapter 6, all headteachers maintained an overview of the curriculum but the amount of their direct practical involvement in review, planning, teaching and evaluating the curriculum differed enormously. Consequently the power to initiate action and the volume of work for deputies, who variously described themselves as 'curriculum leaders', 'assisting the head', 'working in partnership with the head' or 'working alongside the head', also varied considerably. Harrison and Gill (1992) argue that there are strong reasons for the deputy becoming 'director of curricular studies' because of their credibility as fellow teachers, experience of implementing curriculum initiatives and possibility of serving as models through their subject and other responsibilities. They view such a role as particularly appropriate to those deputies whose commitment to teaching has caused them to reject trying for promotion which would take them away from the classroom. However, Harrison and Gill (1992) acknowledge that opportunities would need to be found to give such deputies an overview of practice across the school.

The desire to get into classrooms to familiarize themselves with the practice of other teachers, to work alongside them to develop their approaches to teaching or to monitor the implementation of policies was a recurrent theme among deputies, as it was with curriculum coordinators:

> I do feel that I don't get in the classrooms enough. I think the way we work as a whole school we do have more opportunity to monitor without necessarily going into classrooms because we have a lot of staff discussion about our whole school project and liaising with John as well. I think that I probably am aware of the rhetoric more than the practice but I do try to go in. If I have got a student, I'll go in and work for five or 10 minutes – just talk to the children and as this term I have had support on two days a week I have gone in and chatted with children. I think that staff appreciate that in a way because it shows someone else is interested in what they are doing. They like to share what they are doing. I'd like to do more of that but I'm sure you are hearing that time and again.
>
> (deputy head with no regular non-contact time,
> primary school, 158 pupils)

The majority of deputies had to find ways other than by classroom observation of informing themselves about what was happening in classrooms, which included using opportunities created by students, discussion with teachers in 'snatched time', through listening to staffroom conversations and by 'popping in classrooms where possible'. Examining the pupils' work on display in classrooms and scrutinizing teachers' short term plans were other common strategies. One deputy explained how through analysing teachers' short term plans he could identify difficulties with subject coverage or classroom organization and assist teachers to overcome these by providing additional subject support, resources or coordinator help with activities. Through this process and subsequent discussion with individual teachers, he considered that it was possible to monitor the success of the school's four-year KS2 programme.

Relationships with staff

The deputies in Mortimore *et al.*'s (1988) research emphasized the importance of interpersonal relationships including those with staff. This was echoed in Purvis and Dennison's (1993: 17) survey as they found that the 'socio-emotional role' as 'an encourager or a counsellor to the staff' was viewed as a major part of their role. As discussed in Chapter 6, headteachers increasingly assumed the role of staff counsellor. Perhaps because of this, deputies in the sample did not portray themselves as providing more emotional support for staff than did their colleagues. They supported them in practical ways through doing menial tasks for them, such as photocopying worksheets or fetching project collections from the library. Also, either as part of their role specification or informally, they gave advice and assistance with discipline, pastoral care and special educational needs. However they emphasized their 'encourager', 'communicator' role as they saw it as very important to acknowledge staff strengths and to praise them. Assemblies taken by teachers and their classes and displays of children's work afforded particular opportunities to demonstrate their appreciation of colleagues' efforts.

The deputies all saw promoting good channels of communication as a vital part of their role:

> Communication is very important so everybody knows what is going on. I either tell them one by one or put it in the staffroom. I'm responsible for the staffroom and for the notice boards. One is rotas and timetables and long term issues and then there is a sort of pillar on which goes immediate issues or short term issues. You know, if someone needs to know something that is happening tomorrow I'll put it up and staff have got accustomed to looking there for anything urgent . . . Then in the staffroom there is quite a big week's diary of

events and I fill that in for each week. In it are permanent things and then after that in a different colour I put the week to week issues.

(primary school, 158 pupils)

In addition to notices in the staffroom and directly passing on information to individuals either before or after school, written notes were also passed from classroom to classroom. Apart from aiding the smooth running of the school, keeping staff up-to-date with events and/or policy developments at senior management level was viewed as important to prevent teachers from feeling 'left out' or 'kept in the dark', which could give rise to unnecessary anxiety or irritation and foster resentment. If something arose which was likely to prove sensitive for some or all staff, then deputies would generally ensure that they saw colleagues individually to discuss issues even if they were to be raised later in a meeting of the whole staff.

As part of their communicator role, deputies exchanged information from 'one side to the other'. A valuable asset of being a full time classteacher was the ability both to anticipate classteachers' reactions to proposed changes favoured by the head and to present these changes to colleagues in a way that took account of likely classroom concerns:

If things do occur with staff I can help or elaborate. Sometimes, as you'll realize from talking with him [the headteacher], there's so many diverse things he is involved with, whereas I can relate more to what classteachers want to know because I am in the classroom.

(primary school deputy head)

Some deputies viewed themselves as occupying the middle position between the head and the staff, acting as a mediator for teachers' suggestions:

I feel that it's quite an important role to be a go-between between the head and the staff, although I think that he's very approachable and staff feel that they can go to him. They're not frightened and come to me because they daren't tell him things, but occasionally they do – they say 'Well you tell him because you might get through to him better than I would'. I think that it's important for both of us to be approachable. I don't think it should be just me that sort of is there in the middle but sometimes I do feel like pig-in-the-middle between the head and the staff.

(primary school, 270 pupils)

Where the deputy was simultaneously perceived as 'one of us' and having a close relationship with the head, some teachers considered the deputies were more likely than they to influence the heads' opinions. Of the deputies who did not mention spontaneously such mediation as part of their role, a few, when asked specifically to comment on it, thought it inappropriate:

> At no time do staff use me as a go-between but that's probably because when we set out as a fairly new staff it wasn't necessary. That's not to say that people don't talk to me but they wouldn't expect me to pass on their feelings to Julie. They would go to her themselves.

> (junior school, 250 pupils)

However, a few deputies, who had been in post for several years, added caveats to the fact that this had been their function with previous heads but currently the ones with whom they worked were 'more approachable' which, in line with current advice, perhaps reflects a change in heads' management styles. A question, raised by patterns in the data but outside its agenda, was how far female staff in schools with male heads made greater use of female deputies as mediators than in situations where the head and the deputy were both female.

In some schools, where deputies were working in partnership with, and closely allied to, the head, they felt that this closeness had a distancing effect on their relationships with other staff. When staff criticized or questioned their head's actions or decisions they felt 'Oh I'm the deputy head, I shouldn't be part of this conversation' or 'They don't really understand, ought I to put the head's point of view?' While still viewing themselves as a link between staff and the head, these deputies saw the emphasis shifting to support for the head rather than acting as a 'classteacher representative' or 'friend of the staff'. This was especially the case where deputies were working as change agents with, and for, the head. Thus one deputy explained how the head looked on her appointment as an opportunity to push ahead with changes – including introducing more informal approaches to teaching and greater differentiation – that he had been trying to introduce for some years. She knew staff saw her as 'part of' the head and 'were careful what they said in front of her'. However, she was slowly building up trust among the teachers and was looking forward to having one day a week non-contact time to work alongside them in their classrooms. As she was charged with the responsibility of introducing additional teaching methods she was very conscious of the need to fulfil the role of exemplary classteacher.

In relation to shaping the role and working conditions of other teachers Mortimore *et al.* (1988: 49) found:

> The majority of deputy heads were included in the informal appraisal of their colleagues. In most cases, this took the form of discussions with the headteacher about staff and school development. More than half of the deputy heads interviewed participated in the process of allocating pupils to classes and classes to teachers,

although most of these emphasised that staff preference was also an
important consideration.

This is in contrast to the findings of a questionnaire survey of deputy
heads in 128 primary schools in north Kent (Helps 1993). In relation to the
nine decision making areas addressed by the questionnaire Helps found
deputies largely dissatisfied at too little participation in the decision
making processes within their schools which was:

> most acute in the following areas: budget formulation; the appoint-
> ment of both teaching and non-teaching staff; the allocation of
> allowances to teaching staff; and the allocation of staff to classes and
> of classrooms to staff.

(p. 49)

Some deputies in our sample also had little participation in the
formulation and administration of the budget, but usually felt that this
was justifiable because of their workload and lack of non-contact time.
Generally, deputies in the sample felt that they had influence in
determining the nature of new teaching appointments and the job
descriptions of existing staff. Also, in those schools where heads and
deputies had been appraised, they were involved in the appraisal of
classteachers. Decisions regarding allocation of classes and classrooms
were viewed as determined by the head in negotiation with classteachers,
although the head might seek their opinion.

Relationship with headteacher

The formal responsibilities and informal spheres of influence of deputies
are negotiated with but ultimately controlled by headteachers (see for
example Nias 1987; Southworth 1995). Consequently, deputies' job
satisfaction, effectiveness and personal well-being are largely determined
by their perceptions of, and relationship with, their headteachers. The
condensed nature of our fieldwork obviously makes it impossible to
assess the depth and quality of such relationships between the heads and
deputies in the schools we visited. In the majority of schools positive
messages were conveyed in situations where: heads took deputies' classes
to allow them to be interviewed; issues raised in interviews with one were
related to the other for additional comment; descriptions of school
processes were congruent and heads and deputies agreed on their relative
weaknesses and strengths and spoke warmly of the value of the latter to
them personally and to the school. However, in a few schools the
relationship between the head and the deputy was obviously strained – for
example, in a school with a large number of pupils with emotional and
behavioural difficulties where staff experienced discipline problems. The

deputy felt demoralized and depressed because he considered that what was needed was a carefully worked out whole school policy with an emphasis on rewards for good behaviour whereas the head perceived the problem as largely resting on the deputy's reluctance to take a tough line with difficult pupils.

Following the Staff Relationships in the Primary School Project, Nias *et al.* (1989) argue that headteachers are the founders of their schools' cultures and the deputies in the five project schools, who worked closely with their headteachers, were described as the leading 'culture bearer' (p. 116) securing staff commitment to the school's 'mission' through their actions and example. In our sample we found many cases where deputies had been appointed by their heads who had sought someone of similar educational values and allegiances to assist them in realizing their aims for the school. In a case study of a deputy head's part in the leadership of a nursery and infant school, Nias (1987) portrays her unshakeable loyalty to the head and the ways in which their smooth teamwork was based on a high level of mutual understanding and trust. Deputies in our sample also talked about trying to put policies into practice and setting a 'good' example to staff in diverse aspects of school life, especially in classroom practice.

As deputies had so little non-contact time and, when they did, this was often provided by the head, it was difficult to find opportunities other than before school and at lunchtime for exchanging information and for the head to provide other than rushed snippets of information on aspects of managing the school. Given that deputies spend most of their time teaching, it can be argued that access to office space, a telephone and the school's computer database is unnecessary. However, when deputies did have time for administrative work they were hindered by lack of these facilities. Interestingly, in only one school was there a desk for the deputy in the headteacher's office.

Harrison and Gill (1992) suggest four alternative management models for sharing responsibilities between the head and the deputy. In Model A the headteacher is 'Director of Finance and Administration' and the deputy 'Director of Curricular Studies'. In Model B the roles are reversed. Model C is a compromise between A and B with head and deputy sharing responsibilities in both areas. The final one, Model D, is to appoint the equivalent of a bursar in order that head and deputy may continue to work in essentially the same way as prior to the ERA. In some of the small schools buying into a bursar scheme set up by the LEA meant versions of model D were in operation. Model C predominated especially in medium size schools where deputies, although they mainly held curriculum responsibilities, generally considered themselves to be involved in policy making and the day to day organization and administration of the school. They performed an important function, providing insights and expertise for the head to draw on, 'a sympathetic ear' when problems arose, a sounding board for ideas and companionable moral support in the day to day running of the school.

In larger schools where, as in Model A, heads took responsibility for finance and administration, deputy heads were often members of a senior management team of around four to six people consisting of the head and key stage, phase or year coordinators. If the team was organized hierarchically and the deputies had more non-contact time than the others to carry out whole school responsibilities, they fulfilled a similar role to deputies in smaller schools. However, owing to budget constraints and class size issues in schools, such as a large primary where the two deputies had become classteachers and phase coordinators, deputies were essentially the same as other senior members of staff but with one or more additional responsibilities to justify their status and salary. Schools reorganizing in this way could be regarded as practising 'delayering' (Fowler 1993: 20–23) in terms of 'shortening the links between top management and "front-line" staff' and devolving 'decision-making authority to positions as close as possible to where decisions are implemented'. Heads expect support from all members of the senior management team and they all have a role – if somewhat diluted – as 'culture bearers'. Disbanding the post of deputy to reduce managerial overheads may be a path that some heads decide to follow. In the head's absence one of the senior management team could be paid a deputizing allowance.

Sometimes shared responsibilities with the head led to problems. These arose where the responsibility was allocated to the deputy but in practice carried out by the head or vice versa or where overlap meant that both were likely to tackle the same task – perhaps adopting different approaches – or to consider tasks as part of the role of the other. Several deputies spoke of the uncertainty created in situations of shared responsibility owing to lack of access to people or information. For example, one deputy found the experience of sharing responsibility for SEN with the head unsatisfactory because, while classteachers referred children to her, the headteacher carried out the liaison between parents and outside agencies. However, following the drawing up of staff job descriptions and looking at the school SEN policy, they sought to clarify and develop her role in relation to coordinating approaches to SEN across the school while the head continued to work with parents and outside agencies. As argued by Nias (1987: 52), the development of partnership between heads and deputies requires tolerance on the part of both participants and 'the emphasis of management training for either post must be upon the development of personal and interpersonal qualities and skills such as sensitivity, empathy, flexibility and the capacity to see a situation from another's viewpoint'.

Taking over the school

Nearly three-quarters of the deputy headteachers in Mortimore *et al.*'s (1988) study reported taking over the headteacher's role if he or she were away. These duties were characterized in terms of 'taking assemblies and dealing with parents' queries'. Given the increasing complexity of running a school since the ERA, taking over in the head's absence is now much more demanding than at the time of Mortimore *et al.*'s research. As expressed by one deputy of a junior school (243 pupils):

> It's difficult because you are one of the team and in the classroom 100 per cent of the time and your classroom teaching has obviously got to be of a high standard so you can't let that slip, not that you would want to, but at the same time the pressure is there to be capable of taking over from the head at any given moment and it's very difficult. There's been so much change recently for heads to take in, especially LMS, that they've been trained up to the hilt and all the resources have gone to training them and the deputy heads have been overlooked.

Deputy headteachers in our sample generally felt confident about taking over the school in relation to managing the curriculum, supporting staff and liaising with parents as these areas were already a major part of their role. However, there was concern among deputies who had little or no experience of, or training in, management and administration, that if for any reason the head was away for a week or more, they would find it very difficult to take over the running of the school. Those deputies, who had received training and with whom the head shared what was involved and/or where the secretarial staff were regarded as extremely competent, felt that they would soon learn how to cope. Greatest uncertainty was expressed in relation to problems that might arise in terms of maintaining the premises and school services and over administrative details, such as 'Who do you pay the bus cheque to?' The other area most commonly cited by deputies as unfamiliar was working with governors, with the few exceptions of deputies who were teacher governors or had been involved in school or cluster governor training initiatives.

Heads endorsed the need for deputies to be capable of taking over their role. A middle school head, who had been appointed to his school following the long term illness of his predecessor, described how, as the deputy had been given little responsibility and status within the school he did not have the knowledge or skills necessary to provide leadership. Consequently, when the head took over, the school was behind in National Curriculum planning and assessment and other national initiatives. However, as the deputy of a large junior school put it, if the head provided strong leadership and you were uncertain how long you were likely to be standing in for him or her, whatever your experience or abilities there were considerable limitations on what could be achieved. Drawing on his experience of being a 'minder' he explained:

> There are developments that you would like to do yourself but you can't do them in case you start to do them and then you are not head any more and the head doesn't quite agree . . . In that role as temporary head you are in a holding role trying to maintain everything and stop it going backwards. When you came in as a support certain structures are already there and you have to decide what new roads to go down and the answer is probably not many. In the situation we are in where the head has been away for nearly a year that's where you start to get difficulties because if you have not gone down any new roads the school can't develop.

In-service training and support networks

Despite their heavy workload most deputies appeared to enjoy considerable job satisfaction derived from the relationship with their pupils that they were able to develop as full time classteachers and from the knowledge that they were influential in aspects of school policy making. The impression conveyed during the research was that while on the one hand the range of demands of the job was exhausting, on the other hand the potential for understanding both practice and policy and gaining the respect of both staff and the head gave them a very positive self-image and fuelled their commitment to their work. Like Nias (1987), we also found that our research challenged the perception in the sparse literature available of primary deputies as powerless and ineffectual. Generally deputies appeared to make an extremely valuable contribution to the smooth running of the school, the morale of both the head and other staff and, since the ERA, to make an increasing contribution to the management of the school especially in relation to the development of the curriculum.

Some deputies had no intention of applying to become heads because they did not wish to exchange their work with children for a predominantly financial and administrative role. However, the majority thought that they would seek headship:

> I think you have to accept that you want to be a head. I think that's quite important . . . It's definitely a preparation for headship. So from my own point of view I sort of see myself as a sort of assistant head in a way, but trying to gain experience of what headship would be like and trying to get into all aspects of the working of the school,

so I feel I can cope with the time when it comes when I apply for headship.

The Thomas Committee (ILEA 1985: 67), who believed that 'nearly all deputy heads should be on the way to becoming heads', advocated that they should 'in the course of time, have experience of the various tasks for which heads are responsible'. Deputies considered that having heads provide them with access in school to what was involved in financial management, administration and working with governing bodies, together with opportunities to attend appropriate courses, was vital preparation for headship.

The in-service training received by deputies varied enormously according to the length of time that they had been in post and the importance the LEA attached to training deputies. Hence one deputy described how he had been on a course in 1982 when he was first appointed, another mid-term and one about four years previously addressing National Curriculum implementation. More recently he had been on LMS training. Courses were mainly instigated by LEAs, for example in one LEA 12 headteachers in cooperation with a senior primary adviser planned and delivered a course for senior management which was mainly attended by new deputies. As a result of such induction courses, some deputies kept in touch, such as a group from another LEA that came together once every half term 'usually in a local pub to swap concerns, ideas and policy documents'. A few deputies had been on courses run by private consultants in which deputies drawn from several LEAs received training in headship interviews, working with governors, marketing the school, monitoring the curriculum and other aspects of management. At the time of the second round of interviews a glance through the brochures of the restructured LEA curriculum support and advisory services and the advertisements for courses in the *Times Educational Supplement* (*TES*) revealed recognition of the potential market for courses on deputy headship.

Establishing deputy head support groups within the locality, clusters or pyramids was viewed as difficult because the varying size of the schools concerned and the range of roles fulfilled by deputy heads meant that they had little common ground. However, deputies in one LEA spoke enthusiastically about the support network operating, which was county funded and run by an adviser, and they regretted very much that with LEA restructuring this was likely to cease. Some deputies described how they received support and opportunities for professional development from other networks. For example, one LEA held meetings for curriculum coordinators with responsibility for coordinating and overseeing curriculum development throughout the school and these happened to be predominantly deputies. This group was viewed as a productive forum for discussing current issues and a valuable vehicle for professional development through its guest speaker programme.

It is extremely important that deputies should gradually be introduced to all aspects of managing the school in order to know exactly what is happening, to make a full contribution to the life of the school, to cover competently during the absence of headteachers and to be prepared adequately to apply for headships where they are likely to be in competition with existing heads. However, deputy headship is an important position in its own right and not just a stage en route to headship. Therefore, as West (1992) argues, a deputy should be provided with development opportunities, the head should act as mentor to the deputy and the deputy, through sharing 'the arts of headship' (p. 54), should be in a position to contribute to the learning of the head. Heads and deputies need to agree on the aspects of headship to be covered in school-based training and draw up an agenda for the year. However, as experienced by deputies in our sample, it is very difficult to participate in budget management, curriculum monitoring and working with parents if they have little or no non-contact time. If funds are available, heads may hire regular supply cover for their deputy, which both releases the deputy from class teaching and enables the head and deputy to tackle some tasks cooperatively. It may also be possible to arrange for deputies to spend a few days during the year shadowing deputies and/or heads in other schools in order to increase their understanding of the possibilities of the role and to gain ideas of alternative approaches to meeting their responsibilities. However, with increasing demands on their budgets, heads and deputies are likely to regard such expenditure as an unnecessary luxury.

In order for deputies to widen their experience, develop new skills and knowledge and raise their status with staff and parents, headteachers could consider job sharing with their deputies for two days a week (Kuyser 1994) or exchanging roles every other week on a temporary or permanent basis (Haigh 1994b) or some other form of job rotation which might involve other teachers (Southworth 1994). In the exchange researched by Southworth (1994) the deputy became acting head for one school year, a B allowance postholder became acting deputy head and the head became a classteacher – an 'in-school secondment' to the classroom. Rotating jobs did pose some difficulties; for example the acting head had to become adjusted to her new responsibilities before she could ad-equately support her deputy, which initially inhibited the deputy's development. However, the experience was regarded by all three participants as immensely useful and fulfilled the expectations of the deputy who became fully aware of the workings of the school and prepared to fulfil a wider management brief.

A more modest experiment, such as that reported by Haigh (1994b), where the head and deputy shared the teaching of a Year 4 and 5 class on a one-week-on/one-week-off basis, might be more feasible. As demonstrated by headteachers of small schools in our portrayal of subject specialist teaching in Chapter 3, the potential difficulties of an exchange involved in sharing a class can be overcome and the children benefit from access to teachers with different aptitudes and specialisms. The need for liaison about the curriculum can be minimized and continuity for the children preserved by partners in the jobshare identifying specific areas of the curriculum to emphasize. Such an exchange could also enable headteachers to update their classroom experience protected from interruptions. This could be beneficial since we found that headteachers who had not had a class or regular timetabled teaching commitments for several years were feeling deskilled and out of touch with the demands of the National Curriculum and its assessment. Some deputies may be reluctant to try an exchange because of the increase in workload and responsibility involved and because of their class commitments, and many heads may be reluctant to relinquish power and to channel time and energy into re-establishing their classroom skills. However, the potential mutual benefits should make more heads and deputies willing to experiment.

six

The changing role of the headteacher

Alexander *et al.* (1992: 46) are adamant that primary headteachers 'must take the leading role in ensuring the quality of curricular provision and they cannot do this without involving themselves directly and centrally in the planning, transaction and evaluation of the curriculum'. Past and present manuals for headteachers contain plentiful advice on how to fulfil the role of curriculum leader (for example, Whitaker 1983; Hill 1989; Day *et al.* 1990, 1993). However, research on the role of the primary school headteacher shortly after the implementation of the ERA reveals fears that increasing pressures from management and administration will dilute their curriculum leadership role (see for example, Acker 1990b; Boydell 1990; Hellawell 1991; Jones and Hayes 1991; Laws and Dennison 1991). There appears to be a tension in the role of the headteacher in the wake of more recent government reforms. Thus, on the one hand, headteachers for whom administrative and budgetary concerns have become all-consuming have been criticized for using local management of schools (LMS) to validate flight from the curriculum (Haigh 1993). On the other hand, teaching heads have been characterized as using class commitments as 'a defence mechanism against some of the managerial pressures' (Hellawell 1991: 322). Given the clear guidelines set down by OFSTED (1994b), where expectations of an extended curriculum leadership role are set out, this is an apposite time in which to reassess the changing role of the primary school headteacher.

Local management of schools and administration

We begin with our findings concerning the impact of the implementation of LMS. While most heads welcomed the greater control that this had given them over their schools, it was nevertheless viewed as having profound implications for their roles because, as one put it, 'we have become businessmen – there's no two ways about it – that means the curriculum is just part of my job now'. Successfully managing the school's budget was viewed as a central, and in some cases the central, part of a head's job. During the first round of interviews several of the heads were able to point to improvements to buildings, resources, furnishings and staffing that in the early days of budget delegation they had been able to make:

> Since we have had our own budget the school has been completely redecorated inside, we have replaced quite a few pieces of equipment which were getting old. We've improved a lot of the fabric of the school such as the hall curtains for which there was never any money through the old county scheme, so I think we have now just about completed the interior work of the school.
>
> (headteacher, primary school, 543 pupils)

However, by the second round of interviews heads spoke of the problems of budget cuts and their adverse effects, especially on staffing. For example, the head of a primary school (470 pupils) explained that under LMS she had had to cut back on staffing which she had accomplished by not replacing a member of staff and putting the 'floating' deputy back into a class full time. A few heads also complained of the lack of flexibility under delegated funding to cope with changes in pupil numbers. As one primary school head explained:

> In the old days when the LEA paid salaries, if we reached a certain number of pupils we could get on the phone but now if the money is not there you can't do it. September a year ago, we were expecting 124 children, as the RAF base closed, but they filled the quarters up with extra personnel from all over the place and so instead of less children we had an influx. By January we had 140 and all that term we had no funding to put the staffing up. All we did was put my part time hours up from .3 to .5. We also put in some more NTA hours as it's cheaper. Marion was in her first year and she had 38 in her class of Y[Year]5 and Y6, whereas in the old days the county would have seen our dilemma and sorted it.

Despite media criticisms of headteachers for underspending, several spoke of the need to build up financial reserves for emergencies, in order to retain staffing as long as possible if pupil numbers dropped and to take account of major repairs or redecoration of the school buildings.

As the greater part of the delegated budget was given over to staff salaries (usually around 86 per cent), decisions on how the rest was to be spent and the actual preparation of a budget document were not considered generally to be particularly demanding, given the growing familiarity with budget planning and computer systems for budget monitoring. However, several headteachers felt that more information on the range of services and products available and opportunities to share experiences with other heads would be helpful. All the headteachers spoke of the greatly increased burden of routine administration associated with LMS. In this respect, several headteachers spoke of the vital role played by their secretaries in managing LMS and thereby freeing up their time for other commitments, whilst others were using the services of a peripatetic bursar.

Headteachers of schools housed in old buildings spoke of the disproportionate amount of time they were spending on dealing with, for example, 'leaking roofs', 'dry rot', 'rewiring', 'decoration of the inside and the outside of the building' and the 'installation of security systems'. Apart from repairs and maintenance to school buildings a considerable amount of their time was taken up overseeing catering services, maintenance of the grounds and cleaning arrangements (see Blease and Lever 1992, for similar findings). The head of a large school, where there were sufficient teachers to take on both curricular and other responsibilities, had decided to delegate responsibility for premises:

> What I find is that I spend too much time – particularly on premises issues – bogged down in here [his office]. So I've handed the premises to the old D allowance – he's shed a curricular responsibility and taken a premises one. Now that to my mind is the biggest area of management in the school after the curriculum. There's a lot in it, but we have a good site manager who does the day-to-day work.

Other headteachers also acknowledged the value of competent committed caretakers/site managers who were quick to identify potential problems, to take initiatives to deal with these and to be visible around the school out of school hours to deter vandalism. The supporting role played by the various auxiliary staff has always assisted the smooth running of schools but now their contribution is proving increasingly vital in saving costs, promoting efficiency and allowing heads to devote their time to managing learning rather than managing paperwork, premises and services.

Disturbance handling

As Paisey and Paisey (1987: 134) observe, 'the underlying anxiety about the use of time for headteachers arises from an awareness of the incongruence between what they ought to be doing and what they are doing'. The heads in our sample frequently voiced such an anxiety as they found a great deal of time was spent on unplanned interactions and events and it was individual work to be carried out by them, which did not have a specified protected time slot, that got put off to another occasion or taken home to do. Although as a result of LMS there were increasing numbers of interruptions from those involved in selling or providing equipment, goods and services, as is discussed later in this chapter, an ever growing number arose from having an 'open door policy' for parents. Also, schools situated in communities affected by high unemployment and social deprivation experienced an extremely large number of disruptions related to petty crime in the area and theft and vandalism on the school premises. Such incidents, which headteachers reported to us were becoming very much more prevalent, tended to go in waves and were demoralizing for staff and often extremely expensive. One head described how thieves had lifted out a large photocopier through a ceiling skylight window. Whereas prior to the ERA negotiating with firms to carry out repairs, replace equipment and install security devices would have been managed by the LEA, these matters are now part of the remit of headteachers.

All too frequently vandalism to the premises meant a disruptive start to the day as illustrated by the following account:

> I pulled the car in the drive to find somebody had pulled the gate off. I got the car parked up and a member of staff walked past me from her own car – they've got a problem as their child was ill last night and they've got to go off to the doctor with the child and the teacher won't be in. So by the time I've got to the school door I'm already dealing with a class of kids who haven't got a teacher and a school gate hanging off. I get into the building; the caretaker has found other damage all around – shattered light bulbs and goodness knows what – and was busy trying to mop up glass. At the same time it had been a very frosty morning and the path – we have a particular problem over a school path – hasn't been gritted. The next minute I had a posse of parents screaming and shouting outside the office here holding me to account for the fact that we hadn't gritted the school path. Of course at the same time the police car arrived because the caretaker was trying to report all the damage from the night before. Then two minutes later another mother came in with a child who had actually slipped on this bit of ice and cut its lip. All this before

about 25 to nine. Then I'm trying to sort of placate these parents and sort out the injured child. Staff are busy arriving and I'm trying to grab members of staff and say 'Can we do x, y or z about this class that hasn't got a teacher?' and 'What are we going to do about this class over here which has got a teacher but nowhere to go?' And I mean this is what some days are like. You can find yourself in this whirlpool – maelstrom is the word – of, you know, pure crisis management.

(headteacher, primary school)

Perhaps, unsurprisingly, the headteacher quoted above found that it was extremely difficult during the school day to achieve the work planned, which resulted in the bulk of it being taken home after school and a build-up of tasks to be tackled in the holidays. While it was 'frustrating to get to the end of a week without achieving what you had set out to do', managing difficult and disruptive incidents and common disturbances – such as unexpected visitors, pupil or staff illness, changes in arrangements and the breakdown of equipment – were viewed as a necessary part of a headteacher's role.

Coulson (1986: 36) in his examination of the work of headteachers, comments:

Acting as the school's principal disturbance-handler is a prominent and essential part of the head's task of organisational maintenance. By bearing the brunt of this task he [*sic*] enables his teaching colleagues to go about their work, the principal work of the school, with a minimum of distraction.

Coulson questions how far 'so-called "disturbances" should be regarded negatively as disruptions to routine and stability as opposed to their being accepted positively as a normal and integral part of management' (p. 36). As they seem likely to increase rather than diminish, it appears necessary to acknowledge these disruptions as routine occurrences. However, while the more serious and contentious ones certainly require the headteacher's attention, other low level tasks, which receive headteachers' attention because of their availability, could be dealt with by someone else. Secretaries especially, and sometimes non-teaching assistants, do often field routine enquiries and visits but they also have work to do and often do not have the authority required to make spontaneous decisions.

Working with parents and the community

The publication of the Plowden report (CACE 1967), which stressed the importance of home-school links in the primary school, laid the basis for a rhetoric of greater parental involvement that grew unchallenged throughout the 1970s and 1980s. Successive educational reports sponsored by the government (such as the Warnock (DES 1978b), Taylor (DES/Welsh Office 1977) and Elton (DES 1989c) reports) highlighted the need for more effective parent–teacher relationships and a major research study of primary school effectiveness (Mortimore *et al.* 1988) concluded that parental involvement was a key factor. However, during these two decades there was a shift in the educational rationale for parental involvement in primary schools from viewing it as part of compensatory education where 'deprived' parents who posed problems were to be inducted into the school's values, to a stress on the importance of partnership, whereby schools should be as prepared to adjust to the needs of parents as vice versa (for further discussion of this issue, see Webb and Vulliamy 1996). This theme of parental partnership, with schools being willing to listen to parents and value their contributions, became strongly embedded in the educational literature. It is evidenced not only in accounts of 'good practice' (see for example, Atkin *et al.* 1988) and in more general books promoting parental involvement (see for example, Stacey 1991), but also in national research studies with, for example, Jowett *et al.* (1991: 138) arguing that 'work with parents should be viewed as an integral part of the way schools and services function' rather than as a peripheral 'extra' or optional activity.

If a move from 'parents as problems' to 'parents as partners' characterized the educational rhetoric of the 1970s and 1980s, a further move to 'parents as consumers' characterizes the 1990s. The origins of this lie in New Right educational ideology (Ball 1990c) and its practical manifestations are to be found in recent government reforms with their emphasis upon promoting competition through open enrolment and opting out. Parents' abilities to make informed choices in this competitive market are to be enhanced by their 'right to know' enshrined in the 'Parent's Charter', as discussed in Chapter 1. Legislative changes have also resulted in increased parental representation on governing bodies, which have themselves had to take on greater responsibilities for school policy and management. It is against this background of shifting emphases in the promotion of parental involvement in schools that we consider the implications of some of our research findings.

We found that most schools were expanding the range of ways in which parents were involved in the life of the school. These included: encouraging volunteer helpers in the school library, the classroom and on school visits; organizing National Curriculum meetings and workshops; setting up paired reading schemes; holding painting and repairing weekends, evenings of family entertainment and fund-raising events. Improvements were also being made in the dissemination of information to parents about the school and their children's progress. This was being done through more detailed school brochures, school newsletters, leaflets on curriculum initiatives, school calendars, displays specifically for parents, pupil homework diaries and the involvement of parents in their children's record of achievement. Several heads also enthused about the contribution to teaching the National Curriculum that the expertise of some parents had enabled them to make, especially in the areas of art, music, cookery, information technology, environmental education, games and swimming.

Some schools also had a high profile in their local communities because the premises were in use every evening for a variety of clubs such as scouts, karate, slimmers and Mothers' Union meetings. While placing schools at the heart of the community and increasing local support for them, this usage also gave rise to difficulties and generated additional work for headteachers. They sometimes found themselves coordinating the activities of disparate groups, some of which left classrooms requiring considerable attention before they could be used again for teaching.

A growing area of headteachers' work with parents was meeting with prospective parents to provide them with information about the school. The number of enquiries concerning pupils of all ages, rather than just those about to enter the reception class was slowly but steadily growing and parents expected to be given individual attention by the head, sometimes on more than one occasion. In one small school visited, all the children in Year 5 and Year 6 had been trained to show visitors around the school, which they did with thoroughness and enthusiasm. However, while this was an opportunity for them to develop their communication skills and saved the headteacher's time, if the parents were attracted by what they saw, the teaching head still had to make an appointment after school to discuss their queries with them. A disadvantage of schools entering the market place is that potential customers have to be accommodated and traditionally there is no member of staff, or auxiliary, for whom such work is part of their role. A further consequence of open enrolment is that heads were spending more time in marketing their schools, sometimes with glossy brochures, and in fund-raising.

The headteacher as social worker

Headteachers constantly referred to visits by parents either to discuss their children's difficulties, which often led into discussion of their own problems, or specifically to confide in someone about their troubles and seek help. For example, one junior school headteacher's account of her week prior to the interview contained three references to demanding interactions with parents of a kind that commonly occurred. First, social services called her on Monday morning concerning a complaint by one mother about the way another mother was treating her daughter, which resulted in the head releasing the latter's phone number and then discussing the situation with her as she happened to come into school for another purpose. Second, on Wednesday afternoon the head had a very difficult meeting with a mother 'who was at her wit's end' because her son who had leukemia also had severe behavioural problems. Third, on Friday lunchtime the father of a boy, whose parents were separated, came in and asked to see him. The head knew that there had been family friction but that the father was not prevented access to his son, so she fetched the boy for him and asked to be present during the meeting. She then saw the mother later to explain what she had done. As the head put it:

> Keeping schools on an even keel is so hard, it really is, and it is getting harder. To many people a head, especially a woman head, is often the only professional that you have such easy access to. Most of the time if somebody walks in here I can see them because if I am working on school business or working with my deputy I can shelve it. It's only if I already have someone with me that I can't. If a parent comes in then I'll see them and they know that and the need is growing . . . I mean we have just had a parent killed on the bypass. It's been horrendous. A mum there has needed somebody. You know 12 hours after her husband was killed she was sitting there. Where do you find the words at quarter to nine in the morning? It takes it out of you – the emotional side of it is so difficult.

Headteachers through experience had developed skills in counselling parents and had the information they needed about which agencies they should turn to for further counselling or practical help. Some heads felt that fulfilling this growing need among parents was considerably adding to their workload, but that it was extremely difficult to refuse to provide such support and to do so would cause additional distress for the children:

> To a certain extent perhaps we've been our own worst enemies. You see when schools didn't have this structure, this tightness over curriculum, bureaucracy and all this documentation and when schools didn't have their own budgets, they could afford to spend time having the head as the mother or father confessor figure to people's marriage problems and all the rest of it. Now it looks as if you are pushing people away and the difficulty is, anyone who is a caring person knows full well that if the parents have got problems it inevitably feeds itself down to the kids and you're trying to tackle both things at once.

In a climate of growing social problems owing to the interrelated factors of unemployment, increase in petty crime, drug abuse and family breakdown, schools often provide the most readily available and

accessible source of counselling and information. The likelihood of this is
further increased by the fact that in recognition of the fundamental role
parents now play in their children's education schools are making them
increasingly welcome. For example, in one first school a parents' room
was provided with desks, comfortable chairs, sewing machines and
newspapers to encourage parents, many of whom were from ethnic
minorities, to feel relaxed in the school and to meet one another. When
parents are visiting schools and/or contributing to their activities, if
schools have succeeded in establishing trusting relationships with their
parents, then headteachers and classteachers are likely to be called upon
for assistance in times of difficulty. While classteachers, particularly of the
younger children, are likely to be asked for help when parents bring in
and collect their children from school, such burdens fall dispropor-
tionately on headteachers since, in all but the smallest schools in our
sample, it was only they who had extensive non-contact time.

For many heads in our sample, interaction with parents, some of which
took the form of counselling, represented the most time-consuming
aspect of their role. And yet this aspect of a head's job appears to be totally
ignored, not only in books promoting parental involvement and
management manuals for headteachers (see for example, Atkin *et al*. 1988;
Harrison and Gill 1992), but also in OFSTED's (1993b) *Handbook for the
Inspection of Schools* and in their reports (see for example, OFSTED 1995).
Moreover, throughout the extensive literature promoting the need for
parental involvement in schools, the potential problems of heads having
to act as untrained social workers are only very rarely and briefly alluded
to (for example, Stacey 1991: 53). In this, there appears to have been a
marked change since both the Plowden Report in 1967 (CACE 1967) and
the Seebohm Report (DHSS 1968) in 1968 on the reorganization of the
social services advocated closer liaison between teachers and social
workers.

The neglect of a consideration of the primary headteacher as social
worker in both recent research and in books on parental involvement is
the more remarkable because this issue was a key finding in the first
national survey of parental involvement in primary schools carried out
from 1976–78 (Cyster *et al*. 1979). They noted that 'the large numbers of
head-teachers (80 per cent) who discuss parents' social or marital
problems with them is surprising' (p. 37). Both their questionnaire
responses and case study data suggested that teachers were becoming
increasingly concerned at the addition of a social worker role to their job:

> Comments such as 'I was trained as a teacher, not as a social worker'
> expressed the ambivalence shown by many teachers to their
> responsibilities to parents as well as to children . . . Many teachers
> may still find it difficult to judge how much time should be spent in

advising parents, time which might be put to better use in educating their children. The resolution of these potential conflicts must surely be a matter of concern for educational decision-makers at all levels.

(Cyster *et al*. 1979: 109)

These 'potential conflicts' appear not to have been addressed since that time; in fact, there seems to have been a conspiracy of silence on the issue. The second national survey of parental involvement in schools carried out 10 years later (Jowett *et al*. 1991) not only fails to mention this problem but makes no reference to the preceding Cyster *et al*. (1979) research at all (despite the fact that both research teams were from the National Foundation for Educational Research). The orientation of recent influential research projects on primary schooling has been such that the research questions have precluded a consideration of this theme. Thus, for example, Campbell and Neil (1994) found that the time spent on parental consultations was on average 70 minutes per week, but their work was focused specifically on classteachers in the context of the National Curriculum; Pollard *et al*.'s (1994) research also looked specifically at curriculum and assessment issues and their chapter on headteachers is concerned primarily with management strategies in relation to these; and Hughes *et al*.'s (1994) research is more concerned with parental perspectives on primary schools and teachers than on teachers' perspectives on parental involvement in their schools. Whilst Chapter 2 of Hughes *et al*.'s book is devoted specifically to 'How headteachers see parents', the fact that this is based upon telephone interviews with a sample of 80 heads, who were asked for their views only about the six issues central to the research project, meant that the social work theme could not be addressed. The advantages in this respect of a more open-ended qualitative research strategy are suggested by the fact that it is only in recent ethnographic accounts of the headteacher's role that we obtain a glimpse of the potential importance of the social work theme. Thus, for example, Acker (1990a: 257) refers to a head spending most of one day on parental marriage guidance counselling instead of on a planned school in-service and Southworth in his intensive study of one head notes that his worst memory of headship was 'spending two days with the parents of a pupil who had died' (1995: 134).

Although there is no research which specifically addresses this issue, it seems very likely that what Cyster *et al*. (1979) identified as a major problem in the late 1970s is an even greater problem now. This is because there is widespread evidence of growing social problems since the early 1980s associated with an increasing gulf between the rich and the poor in Britain (see for example, Andrews and Jacobs 1990). Schemes to provide educational social workers in schools initiated by Education Welfare Services, other LEA community services and voluntary agencies demonstrate the value to the schools of the specialized support that they provide (Jenkins 1994). However, the decline in LEAs and in government resourcing of education and the social services in general has led to a decrease in such support. Thus some LEAs used to employ home–school liaison officers who might have assisted with such parental needs (see for example, Alexander 1992: 94–5). Although one cluster group in our research sample agreed to fund a shared appointment jointly and in another authority home–school liaison officers were going to be funded by City Challenge, such posts appear generally to be becoming an unaffordable luxury under LMS. Similarly Jenkins (1994) reports that the Education Welfare Service, which is staffed by Educational Welfare Officers, many of whom are increasingly seeing their role as shifting from the stereotype of 'truant catchers' to one of providing preventative social work, has been cut back over the past decade. The scale of the 'headteacher as social worker' problem, coupled with the lack of attention to it in the recent educational literature, perhaps explains why it attracted considerable media attention when the report of our research was first published. The Association of Teachers and Lecturers endorsed a call to the government to provide funding for school-based social workers in primary schools in deprived areas (Hofkins 1994) – a move which placed the issue firmly on the public agenda (see, for example, MacLeod 1994; Judd 1994).

Relationships with governors

In her *Times Educational Supplement* (*TES*) lecture delivered at the 1994 Education Show in Birmingham Joan Sallis outlined the awesome task faced by governors in assuming their responsibilities:

> to build productive relationships with staff; to cope with the workload and the jargon; to organise their time; to develop as an effective team with no powerful groups taking over; to keep upright on the shifting sands of law and regulations.
>
> (reported in the *TES*, 18 March 1994: 5)

While she considered that a head working in partnership with governors could help them to solve most of the problems encountered in their role, she viewed motivating heads to work towards building genuine partnerships as a major problem. As she appreciated, 'sharing hurts' and heads may be reluctant to acknowledge the inevitable and willingly assist in the relinquishing of power. In the sample schools governor participation could be viewed as on a continuum with at one end governing bodies who did little more than provide moral support – occasionally supplemented with practical assistance and contributions to assemblies – and at the other governing bodies who were empowered to play a growing role in decision making.

The general view of relationships between schools and their governing bodies was that the latter were extremely supportive but that 'they left the day to day handling of the school' to the head and that 'they didn't interfere', 'they didn't intrude'. As one primary school head pointed out, 'the governing body doesn't do what it is required to do by law' and 'we haven't this high powered system of subcommittees, regular meetings and proactive governors'. However, the governors were extremely interested in the life of the school, paid regular visits, gave practical help when asked and, in the case of one parent governor, was in every week working with children as part of a parent support group for the teaching of reading.

In some schools, heads spoke of the difficulties in getting governors to assume their responsibilities. One head of a primary school who described his governing body as 'the salt of the earth', claimed that, although they had received training, what was actually expected of them was outside their experience and interests and that in practice he did the bulk of their work:

> I had to pass a resolution at one of my governors' meetings that actually said 'OK, if these working parties aren't being set up – finance, premises, staffing etc. – if they are not prepared to then they must delegate those responsibilities to the head and I want that in writing'.

However, he tried to get them to appreciate that 'the buck doesn't stop with me – it's a collective corporate responsibility'. More recently, 'the inspection issue has made me realize I can't just go on getting away with running this school fairly autocratically in terms of the governors'. Consequently, he and the deputy were going to try to increase the governors' involvement in decision making by getting them to assist in the production of a policy for educational visits and journeys. At the next meeting they were going to give them headings to work on in small groups and then draw the sections together with the governing body as a whole.

Several schools had put considerable effort into helping governors to be aware of what was required of them and to enable governors and staff to get to know each other. The approaches adopted, if combined, provide useful suggestions as to ways forward:

- if possible, provide opportunities for governors to spend regular time in school assisting with a specific task or subject;
- invite one or a few governors to staff meetings on topics of particular interest to them;
- invite teachers to governors' meetings to explain specific issues;

- provide papers for governors that are short, clear, lively and avoid the use of jargon;
- cooperate with cluster schools to provide training and/or opportunities for governors to discuss their contribution;
- involve governors at the brainstorming stage of developing a policy and then enable them to follow that policy through the documentation and implementation stages;
- use them as a sounding board as to how a new initiative is likely to be received by parents;
- ensure that the deputy head knows the governors and is familiar with current ways of working.

Those heads where partnerships were being developed successfully considered that closer working relationships with governors shared the workload and meant that, in what often seemed dangerous times for heads, accountability was shared.

A small minority of schools had moved a long way towards creating a partnership with governors. One head of a large primary school explained how creating a governing body of able people, who understood what was expected of them and could contribute to the development of the school, had been in the school's development plan:

> The governing body is now set up and running with four main subcommittees all run by experts in their own field. The finance committee is chaired by a bank manager, the buildings committee by the manager of a building society, the staffing subcommittee is chaired by the personnel director of a pet food company and the curriculum subcommittee is chaired by a teacher who has just retired – all people who understand the various aspects of their committee's work. The overall chairman is a consultant at a computer software company. It's quite a high powered governing body. Three other members are graduates in different jobs and then there are two or three parents and so there is a good balance across the community. They all serve on one of the four committees. I find with four subcommittees operating as they do, all the main work is done in these and the main committee meets to rubber stamp.

A major factor in achieving partnership appeared to be how far heads deliberately set out, or were able, to recruit governors with professional expertise whom teachers would respect. However, to work with the 'high powered governing body' described above required a confident head who felt able to manage any situations which might arise if, once the governors had become accustomed to their role, they pushed for policies in opposition to the school's preferred practices.

Supporting staff

All the heads were concerned about the pressures on staff caused by the changes in primary education and the lowering of morale caused by fatigue and the negative characterizations of teachers continually emanating from the media and the government. Echoing the findings on the effects on teachers of the implementation of the National Curriculum at KS1 (Campbell and Neill 1992), headteachers described how staff had experienced considerable anxiety and stress since the introduction of the National Curriculum and that some of their most conscientious teachers were carrying extremely heavy workloads. They spoke of teachers 'getting close to the edge', 'hanging on by their fingernails' and 'sinking under the weight of it all'. Therefore, all the headteachers were concerned to be alert to teachers' physical and mental welfare, to demonstrate their concern, to acknowledge the hard work being done and to find ways of offering support. Thus, like the head in Acker's (1990b: 269) ethnographic case study, some heads felt that, since the ERA, one of their main roles had become that of staff counsellor. As one put it:

> I see my role as carer of the staff because I feel if they're right, everything else will be right. I've got a dozen teaching and non-teaching staff and I do miss things occasionally but I work very hard not to. I talk to every member of staff every day. I consider it so important to say 'How are things?, How was open day last night?, How's your decorating going?' because that way I can feel how they are . . . Our lunchtimes are very special. We normally only get together for 20 minutes but it's a time when I chat. There are some people, they don't know this, but I have parts of days when I talk to different people and I can do it most days.

Many heads said that they tried to visit each class at some point during the day to exchange a greeting with the teachers at the very least:

> I do try and get round seeing all classes each day – that is in my mind when I start off, but unless I do it very early then I can get trapped by social problems. I go around and wish teachers 'Good Morning' and try and pick on something positive, either a child's behaviour or something nice that's happened in the classroom, and greet parents. It would be no more than two or three minutes in each class to get round 10 classes plus the nursery in about half an hour. But I can't pretend it happens every day.
>
> (headteacher, primary school, 270 pupils)

An important way in which this head provided support for his staff was to assist them to manage the emotional and behavioural difficulties experienced by a large number of the school's pupils. Most days would be punctuated with the need for him to provide assistance for teachers in coping with pupils who had truanted or were being disruptive in the classroom (the interview was interrupted by a teacher bringing in a boy who had been waving his penis at other children in the class). The pressure brought about by the overloaded National Curriculum to move pupils swiftly through content meant that classroom disruptions were additionally stressful for teachers as they reduced time for curriculum coverage. There was also a general feeling that, owing to factors such as unemployment, family breakdowns and growing poverty, children were developing more behavioural problems. Consequently, support with such problems from heads and deputies was regarded as important. In common with the head in the above quotation, all the headteachers emphasized the importance of talking informally with staff and often went into the staffroom at breaktimes and/or during lunchtimes. In one large school, where there was less likelihood of regular informal conversations with staff, the head set up a routine whereby he saw a member of staff for half an hour every Monday lunchtime.

Another approach to reduce staff anxiety and maintain morale was to reach whole school understandings about what the school was and was not doing in relation to the National Curriculum and to ensure that governors and parents were aware of this and the reasons behind it. Heads felt that uncertainty and anxiety were lessened considerably if teachers were clear about what was expected of them and knew that parents and governors were aware of the school's limitations and supportive of the ways in which these were being addressed. One headteacher described his approach:

> If teachers are worrying that they are not covering this or that, then they are not going to teach effectively and a lot of energy is used up worrying, so some of my time is spent giving messages saying 'Don't worry if anybody gets upset because we are not covering a particular part of the National Curriculum, be it a parent, an inspector, whoever. Don't worry. They can beat me with a big stick, not you', and that has helped a lot I think. Teachers know anything that we do is overt. Nothing is hidden, we will explain why we haven't done things.

As illustrated in the above quotation, headteachers saw themselves as having a responsibility to protect staff by intercepting any criticisms and fielding these themselves. This was a characteristic of headship that teachers mentioned frequently as of primary importance in the current climate.

Curriculum leadership

Across the 13 LEAs the advisers/inspectors interviewed stressed that strong curriculum leadership by the headteacher characterizes effective schools. They therefore considered that where headteachers were becoming administrators and 'chief executives' they should identify strategies to enable them to regain their curriculum role. However, as admitted in a discussion paper (OFSTED 1994b: 9), this role alone has expanded to involve 'a formidable list of responsibilities', including

> a great deal of focused discussion about the curriculum with colleagues; leading, and contributing to staff and team meetings; developing and reviewing policies; analysing assessment data and children's work; observing teachers and children at work; consulting members of the governing body and others with a concern for the work of the school; keeping up to date with local and national curriculum documentation; and, very importantly, finding time to reflect upon progress and the direction of the work.

It is interesting to consider how far, and in what ways, these expectations were borne out in practice in the schools in our study.

All the headteachers said that they maintained an overview of the curriculum and sought to ensure that the ways in which it was taught were in line with their vision and beliefs. The number and nature of the curriculum activities in which they were involved differed greatly according to the school's management structure, the strengths and weaknesses of deputy headteachers, the number of staff available to act as curriculum coordinators and headteachers' work preferences. However, in all but the smallest schools, the meaning of curriculum leadership was perceived as changing. As one head of a large school with 543 pupils put it:

> To say that the headteacher of a school this size should be the curriculum leader is not what you mean in a primary of 150 pupils. I mean, you are still the curriculum leader in that you have overall responsibility for the implementation of the National Curriculum, but my chief job is to set up the management structures to carry out the wishes of the governing body and myself. In relation to the curriculum, the two most important people after the deputy head are the KS1 and the KS2 coordinators and they are scale C posts and those two people are my eyes and ears really.

A more traditional curriculum leadership role was the dominant one for teaching heads in small schools, because they were primarily concerned with the ways in which it affected their teaching and their daily interactions with children:

> Any ideas that I have that I feel we should be doing – they're never impractical because I know that I've actually got to put them into practice myself in class. It makes me more realistic and I also appreciate the pace of change and try and structure it in a way so that everyone can cope with it.

As they familiarized themselves with the orders, they tried to translate the requirements into classroom practice. More detailed plans and policy statements gradually evolved as, and when, there was time to work on them. Headteachers in small schools tended to view themselves as 'doers' rather than producers of documentation. They felt that it was more important to use time after school to provide extracurricular activities for children and opportunities for parents and governors to become involved in the life of the school than to create policies. As put by the headteacher of a small church school: 'We don't have time to write policy documents – we are too busy doing them'.

Some headteachers regarded 'curriculum leadership as what you were trained for and what you like to do'. Consequently, they tried to engage directly in the review, long and medium term planning, teaching and evaluation of all or some of the National Curriculum subjects. They checked teachers' written short term plans either weekly or fortnightly and regularly examined pupil assessments. Some also led staff meetings on the curriculum and ran or organized INSET days. Retaining an active role in curriculum development was also viewed as promoting good staff relationships and enabling headteachers 'to keep a finger on the pulse of the school':

> I honestly feel that the curriculum is still my most important role. I feel if I were to lose the curriculum I would then lose my best point of contact with the staff and I think I can only run a successful team if I can have a dialogue with them about the things that are really relevant for our children.
>
> (headteacher, 9–13 middle school)

However, as discussed in Chapter 5, most headteachers in other than small schools had delegated aspects of this work to their deputy headteachers and in the largest schools to members of their senior management team. This was partly because of the growing pressures of other aspects of the head's job and also because they felt progressively less competent to undertake them. Thus headteachers who did not have a regular teaching commitment considered that not having first-hand experience of teaching the National Curriculum themselves reduced their ability to provide curriculum leadership in terms of making recommendations and leading by example. As one put it:

> I don't feel I am able to give as positive a lead as I would like to, because I'm not directly involved now with whole class teaching or having a class responsibility. If staff level a criticism at me, 'what does he know about this because he doesn't have to do it?', it could be a fairly valid one. I think the lead needs to come from the member of staff who's actually involved in doing it.

Whilst our data showed progressively less direct involvement by heads in curriculum leadership within their own schools, they showed a greater involvement in curriculum and staff development activities at local and national level. The majority of heads considered that, owing to their participation in course provision and meetings related to the National Curriculum, LMS, appraisal and more recently OFSTED inspections, they were spending increasing amounts of time out of school. In the current situation where schools are responsible for their own INSET and preparing for OFSTED inspections they regarded it as extremely important to make use of available opportunities to find out what was happening in other schools and other authorities, especially in relation to the curriculum and assessment. While this was of benefit to them and their schools, they were also agreed that staff often resented their absence and their lack of availability to provide support when it was needed.

Teaching commitments

The DES discussion paper considers that all headteachers should 'lead by example' when it comes to classroom practice:

> They may not have timetabled teaching commitments, but all headteachers should teach. Actions speak louder than words and the headteachers teaching can and must exemplify their vision of what the school might become.
>
> (Alexander *et al.* 1992: 48)

In his account of the work of primary school headteachers in the decade prior to the ERA, Coulson's (1986: 64–5) observations indicate that headteachers acknowledged the value of following the above advice:

> The readiness of heads to put time in classrooms is highly valued by most teachers. It makes a recognisable area of his work more visible to them and shows a willingness to attempt what he advocates: to 'come down on to the shop floor', 'get his hands dirty' and 'practise what he preaches'. The shouldering by the head of a substantial, if irregular teaching load is usually seen by teachers as beneficial to

staff morale; it serves to underline the importance of the classroom and the activity of teaching among the head's priorities.

The minority of headteachers, in other than small schools, who had a regular teaching commitment certainly regarded it as part of the 'credibility game where you go in and show that you can do it as well as anyone else'. However, headteachers felt that staff had become accustomed to the notion of non-teaching heads and understood why this was necessary. Also, the changing educational and political climate had led to a situation where classteachers valued aspects of the head's role which supported them in their work and explained it to parents, governors and the wider community as much, or even more than, their ability to take a class.

Headteachers in small schools considered that their class responsibilities must have priority over all the other demands of their role. As one teaching head of a small school (65 pupils) explained:

I'm contracted to teach four days a week and that's what I'm going to do and that's where my strength and my energies go. I'm always in school by eight o'clock anyway but there's always something to do – something crops up. But I always ensure I've got my materials ready so, if anything happens, we are ready to go in the classroom. Everything else tends to go by the by.

However, they admitted to ever increasing difficulties as a result of their widening responsibilities in trying to ensure that their classteaching was not interrupted. Headteachers in schools with between 100 and 200 pupils, who had a class commitment, were finding it an increasing struggle to maintain the quality of their teaching:

I think that it is totally wrong that I should be running a six teacher school and have a class commitment for two and a half days. I cannot do it in this day and age of quality control. How can I get in the classrooms? How can I run appraisal? The more children I have does not increase the paperwork by that much, but the more bodies there are, the more parents there are and the more problems there are – many of the problems to be dealt with come from parents . . . My class do suffer from it because I get called out and I have to pin the door open.

Headteachers in larger schools who, although they had no class commitment, taught regularly and considered it important to teach in order to be aware of the demands made on pupils and on classteachers by the implementation of the National Curriculum. Increasingly, heads were operating as supply teachers, when classteachers were absent. Others, whose preferred practice was to get in a supply teacher, felt that the need to save money was likely to mean that increasingly they would be forced to provide supply cover themselves. The need to provide non-contact time for coordinators to fulfil their responsibilities and to familiarize themselves with practice across the school was also placing pressure on heads to teach in order to release teachers from their classrooms.

Many headteachers in our sample, in consultation with staff and governors, had found ways of not having a regular teaching commitment in order to provide additional time for administrative and managerial tasks. The headteacher of a junior school was one of those who found that she simply had no time to have a teaching commitment:

> I can't. I know some people do. I've got over the guilt. I had horrendous guilt because I've come up through the primary system working with teaching heads mainly in village schools. I was a peripatetic head for six years. I won't crisis teach. I won't if somebody is off just go and say 'Oh I'll do it' you know and juggle three balls in the air at the same time. I can't do that.

She also admitted that having been out of the classroom for several terms:

> You also lose the ability to do it. Because the role of the head has changed so much in the last two years for me to actually go in and deliver that now. Although the skills are still there, they're rusty.

Other headteachers also described the deskilling effects of demands of the ERA which pulled them away from the classroom. This was mainly in terms of awareness that they did not have the same knowledge of the orders as their staff, nor the same confidence and experience in teaching the newer aspects of some subjects. Headteachers who have had a period away from the classroom are likely to find it increasingly difficult to regain their confidence and proficiency as exemplary classteachers.

Monitoring

By the second round of interviews headteachers felt that time available to be in classrooms needed to be spent monitoring rather than taking a class or working alongside classteachers in order to develop particular skills. In order to do monitoring systematically and rigorously it was not possible to teach at the same time. The emphasis upon quality assurance was seen by some heads as an important aspect of their role in the future:

> I think the main shift is going to be on looking at what's happening in the school – monitoring – that's what I think we're moving to. We've almost got to take on the inspector's role in the school, particularly a school of this size, because of the nature of the school, someone has got to keep that overview of what is happening and

you can't do that and be involved in all the development issues as well.

(headteacher, primary school, 668 pupils)

Following the completion of our fieldwork, all primary schools have received a copy of a further discussion paper on teaching and learning (OFSTED 1994b) which emphasized the role of the headteacher in monitoring teachers' plans and classroom practice and evaluating all aspects of the whole curriculum and the quality of education provided.

Heads viewed taking on a monitoring role as an immediate priority in order to ensure that school policies and practices were ready to withstand the scrutiny of OFSTED inspections. Increasingly, as discussed in Chapter 4, the criteria for inspection in the OFSTED handbook were being shared with staff and used to assess aspects of the school organization and curriculum. Time available to be spent in classrooms was viewed as needed for observations both to identify weaknesses and to prepare teachers to cope with the anticipated stress of having inspectors in their classroom. One headteacher of a first school (311 pupils) described the kinds of preparations in which her school was engaged:

> I had my inspector come in in May and she has actually monitored four classes for me and my deputy monitored four classes and I monitored four. We were looking at one area – just looking at the maths – and out of that came a need for us to do a lot more monitoring. So I've put the senior management, they're actually having some training in this because they were quite fearful of going into a class and monitoring their colleagues and it's taken a lot of confidence building with the rest of the staff. It's not something we can do overnight – it's a long term plan. I have started doing it in the maths area as from September – it's actually a target I have set myself as part of my appraisal . . . it's very, very hard because as soon as I go into class I want to sit down and work with the children, but that was a criticism on my appraisal that I wanted to get too involved with the children. I wasn't standing back and monitoring what was actually going on in the class – so I've had to learn those skills myself. I only go in for half an hour but the children know that when I am there they do not disturb me. I'm writing and I'm observing all sorts of things that are going on in the maths area . . . I don't want it as a threatening thing but I do want the staff to get used to the fact that when we have an OFSTED inspection that is exactly what the inspectors will do. They'll just stand in a room and monitor what's going on.

Headteachers had discussed OFSTED inspections with their LEA advisers/inspectors, who in some cases as in the above example had carried out what were referred to as 'OFSTED MOTs' of parts of the school curriculum. They had been on courses either provided by their LEAs or private consultants on how to prepare their schools for inspection and in several cases were beginning to prepare the governors, either by personally discussing the inspection process with them or, as a preliminary to this, asking an LEA inspector to give an introductory talk at a governors' meeting. However, although headteachers were trying to take a calm and systematic approach to their preparations, the notion of being inspected, especially early on in the inspection cycle, was an enormous source of pressure and anxiety. Heads were worried that at best the aspects of the school of which the staff were proud might only be rendered 'satisfactory' – a term which had a mediocre ring to it – and at worst that inspectors might take a very critical stance on areas of the curriculum for which there had been inadequate time to give the attention needed. They were also very worried about the effect on staff morale and self-esteem in both the short term while the inspection was taking place and in the long term if the inspection identified too many issues to be addressed. Insecurity was generated by the unknown and, unsurprisingly, fears were fuelled further by the press attention to failing schools.

The new headteacher's role: a recognition of diversity

The role of headteacher has become so diverse, expansive and responsive that although heads work to long term goals there is a sense that 'getting on top of it all' in the short term is impossible. Operating a closed door policy to facilitate the completion of high priority tasks requires a change in attitude on the part of heads and the school community in order to regard this as acceptable. However, clearly heads must seek to minimize distractions from their time for management and administration and secure the support of governors and staff for whatever measures are needed to enable this to happen. The time management of heads needs to stand up to scrutiny because increasingly they determine the tasks and time targets for teachers to whom they have delegated responsibilities.

Curriculum leadership as exercised by headteachers could be characterized as on a continuum from being one of the areas over which heads had a managerial overview at one end to being the main priority for the headteacher's personal attention at the other. For the headteachers who no longer had a regular teaching commitment, their lack of familiarity with the orders and with the translation of these into classroom practice meant that they considered curriculum leadership could be more effectively offered by deputies and curriculum coordinators. While it may be educationally desirable that heads should retain expertise in classteaching, most find it practically impossible in the current situation, with the exception of those in small schools. As suggested in Chapter 5, one solution to regaining that expertise is for the head to participate in job rotation of the kind described by Southworth (1994). The head whom he researched used his year as a classteacher to improve and update his classroom skills, resensitize himself to classroom concerns and devise additional ways of supporting teachers in the classroom. An additional bonus was that the change of role made him feel refreshed and relaxed. However, to undertake such a project requires a head to have confidence in a like-minded deputy, the existence of a stable school environment and the support of staff, governors and parents.

While the climate in which headteachers manage their schools has changed dramatically since the Plowden report, there has been remarkable continuity of expectation at the level of national policy that heads should be curriculum leaders and exemplary teachers (compare, for example, CACE 1967: 332–4 with Alexander *et al*. 1992: 46–9). However, the concept of curriculum leadership has increasingly been redefined and extended to include additional responsibilities and skills, especially in relation to planning, policy making, monitoring and evaluation. Also, as Handy and Aitkin (1986: 35) have pointed out, in other organizations, 'the higher you rise in an organisation the greater the proportion of the managerial element in your life'. It seems unrealistic to expect primary headteachers both to develop the new post-ERA managerial knowledge and skills and to maintain their teaching expertise. The expanding nature of heads' work, together with increasing pressures for them to be cost effective, competitive and measurably efficient managers of their schools, mean that it may have to be accepted that headteachers are likely to become chief executives, rather than trying to run their organizations as operatives on the shop floor. With the exception of small schools, curriculum leadership and teaching skills seem set to continue to be pushed further and further down headteachers' lists of priorities.

At the same time as these demands have increased, so have the wider managerial and administrative requirements resulting from other aspects of the ERA, together with increasing pressures from parents. In addition, the roles and responsibilities of classteachers have also expanded exponentially, placing new expectations upon heads who teach. Hargreaves (1994) aptly depicts the headteacher's dilemma in his characterization of the 'postmodern' school, where 'as the pressures of postmodernity are felt, the teacher's role expands to take on new problems and mandates – though little of the old role is cast aside to make room for these changes' (p. 4). Given this unrealistic and unmanageable workload, headteachers have to make choices about their priorities based on the size, staffing levels and expertise in their schools. An enormous variety in these contextual factors was revealed in our sample schools, suggesting the need for management advice to develop a range of approaches, which recognize that the work of primary headteachers should differ in contrasting circumstances. The acceptance of such potential diversity is currently lacking in OFSTED's (1993b) handbook for the inspection of schools and in their discussion papers (see for example, OFSTED 1994b).

This growing diversity in the managerial roles of primary school headteachers is contributing to a growing diversity in potential occupational identities. Southworth concludes his detailed portrayal of Ron Lacey, the subject of an intensive ethnographic study of one primary school headteacher, by arguing that:

> Headship was not a job, it was a way of life. It was the integration of professional and personal beliefs and experience which were not so much worked out as *lived out* in the school. The school was an extension of him. Thinking about the school filled much of his day and was forever with him.
>
> (1995: 135)

For Ron Lacey, being a headteacher was about leading his staff in the implementation of his vision for the school. The thrust of the external changes challenged this vision, diverted his energies, reduced his power to influence and support colleagues and so threatened his occupational identity (Southworth 1995). Similarly, Peter and Dave, two of the heads in Woods's (1995) study of 12 creative teachers in five primary schools, found the transition from their own interpretation of the role of headteacher to the post-ERA model extremely traumatic – Peter taking early retirement and Dave being forced into it through 'burn-out' and ill health. Building upon Nias's (1989) theory of the centrality of self among primary school teachers, Woods illustrates how they felt that their occupational identities, based upon progressive ideals and close contact with children, were being threatened. As Dave put it:

> The type of thing I was having to do in terms of administration was taking me away from some of the ideals that I got into the job for. I felt that the kind of person they were looking for was somebody completely different. I was not the kind of headteacher that they needed or wanted.
>
> (Woods 1995: 177)

We also found a few headteachers who were contemplating retiring earlier than they had originally envisaged, but they were counterbalanced by others for whom the changes were regarded as offering new possibilities for the development of their schools and an opportunity for professional renewal. These headteachers had either adapted to the post-ERA model or welcomed it because it drew upon their particular interests, strengths or latent skills, providing, especially for those who had been in post for some time, a new phase to their career. Thus whereas Peter who took early retirement complained that the headteacher role was being transformed from that of a 'leading professional' to a 'chief executive' (Woods 1995: 153), we found certain heads who relished this prospect. Moreover, contrary to what might be assumed, some of them held the same kinds of progressive convictions that Woods identifies in his sample of creative teachers. However, having been successful classteachers for many years, they regarded the challenges of managing a large school in the post-ERA climate as exciting new ones, deserving of the same level of personal and professional commitment as they had earlier given to other aspects of the teacher's role.

seven

Managing whole school change in the post-ERA primary school

Throughout the 1980s there was an increasing emphasis upon the management of whole school change in the primary school. It was argued that previously paternalistic and autocratic styles of primary headteachers should give way to more collaborative and collegial approaches to whole school management (Coulson 1980; Campbell 1985). An ideal type emerged whereby all teachers should participate actively in negotiating an agreed curriculum and contribute jointly to planning, implementing and evaluating its delivery (Wallace 1988). This can be witnessed in central and local policy documentation (see for example, DES 1982a, 1985a; ILEA 1985; House of Commons Select Committee 1986), in management texts (see for example, Day *et al.* 1985; Spear 1987), in the literature on school effectiveness and school improvement (see for example, Reid *et al.* 1987; Mortimore *et al.* 1988; Fullan 1992) and in ethnographic studies of 'cultures of collaboration' (Nias *et al.* 1989) and 'whole school curriculum development' (Nias *et al.* 1992) in primary schools. Such aspirations for collaborative approaches to whole school change still pervade much current advice to primary schools, whether from OFSTED (see for example, the emphasis on teamwork in OFSTED 1994a) or from academics (see for example, Fullan and Hargreaves 1992; Whitaker 1993). However, the plethora of innovations associated with the implementation of the ERA have created a climate in primary schools far removed from that of the 1980s from which the current orthodoxy for collaborative whole school development was derived. In this final chapter we examine the impact that recent government-imposed changes have had on the management of change in the primary school and assess to what extent collaborative approaches to the management of whole school change are either possible or desirable in the current climate.

Working together

Research on school effectiveness suggests that:

Where staff had been involved in the development of guidelines for their school, there was likely to be school-wide consistency in guideline usage. Where staff had not been involved, however, there was likely to be variation, with teachers tending to adopt individual approaches to the use of guidelines for different curriculum areas. It appears, therefore, that staff involvement was related to a more consistent school-based approach to the curriculum.

(Mortimore *et al*. 1988: 233)

The implementation of the National Curriculum brought staff together to share anxieties and to plan for change (NCC 1990b; Osborn and Pollard 1991). All the headteachers in our sample spoke of the growth in openness, discussion and cooperation among teachers since the introduction of the National Curriculum. They described a variety of planning meetings at the level of the whole school, key stages and year groups, whole school curriculum events – such as workshops for parents – and in-service days where staff had worked together. Most heads and teachers saw the increase in sharing as legitimated and promoted by the National Curriculum but building on collaborative management structures that were already beginning to be put into place. Others viewed it as the direct result of the need to discuss anxieties and to pull together to resolve problems in order to cope with National Curriculum implementation.

When collective decision making took place, the process gave headteachers valuable access to the views and ideas of their staffs. However, several referred to the time-consuming nature of meetings where 'the discussion phase seemed to go on and on' and 'I felt we weren't getting anywhere'. Some teachers shared this view and most felt that there were too many meetings which ate into their time for lesson planning and preparation – a constraint identified also in Hayes's (1994) case study of a head's attempt to develop a collaborative climate in her school. Sometimes the discussion in meetings exposed fundamental differences in beliefs and practices which could not be resolved. Lack of agreement could lead to a period of non-action until at least partial consensus was arrived at. Also, a few heads had found that, if at the outset of a policy initiative teachers expected to arrive at a decision collectively, it was difficult midway through the process to switch merely to involving and consulting them as this could lead to cynicism or resentment.

In his research with teachers, Hargreaves (1994) found that the necessity to get together at prescribed times in order to tackle work imposed by external requirements often resulted merely in what he characterizes as 'contrived collegiality', or 'a safe administrative simulation of collaboration'. 'It replaces spontaneous, unpredictable and difficult-to-control forms of teacher generated collaboration with forms of collaboration that are captured, contained and contrived by administrators instead' (p. 196). Hargreaves regards such forms of collaboration as inflexible and inefficient and giving only cosmetic empowerment to teachers. The teachers in our sample appeared to be coming to similar conclusions. Consequently, schools were tending to move away from whole school involvement throughout the process of policy production and the implementation of initiatives to giving one or more staff tasks on which to work and involving others at key points to obtain suggestions and evaluative comments.

In situations where differing staff values and resistance to change made attempts to work cooperatively on initiatives unsuccessful, several headteachers spoke of how they had used the National Curriculum as a lever to 'get teachers who had got somewhat set in their ways to start to move' and to introduce changes in the curriculum that they felt were long overdue. As one head put it: 'Because it was down in black and white and it is the law that you have to do it, it's made it considerably easier to effect the kind of changes that were very definitely necessary'. The head of a primary school, who described how he had almost given up trying to bring about change in his school, derived encouragement and power from the legislation:

> I would say three cheers for the National Curriculum because at least it's certainly developed some staff in a way that they'd never have thought possible . . . I took over an existing system where there was no real evidence of progression and continuity and there were some very able people doing their own thing in pockets with no regard whatsoever to what was going before or what came after. I was struggling with members of staff who saw no reason to change. They believed that what they did was right. They didn't believe that what I was trying to suggest was better or even worthwhile doing, so it was taking an enormous amount of my time and they could always come out with an answer that stops you in your tracks. I was trying to lead by example, or persuasion, or encouragement, or a lot of discussion to try to develop their thinking and in two cases not getting very far at all other than having confrontations. You know, I would insist that you do that for six weeks and then we'll evaluate it. Along came the documentation and there all of a sudden I could say 'Right you see that, do it. Not

for me, no, but because the law says we all have to do it', and so that was a major turning point.

Teachers who were hostile to the changes were more likely to target their resentment at the government, rather than at the head and others involved in introducing the changes, which was helpful for staff relationships.

Heads complained that the pace at which the changes were introduced meant that teachers had insufficient time for critical reflection on existing practice, for the collection of evidence on which to base decisions and for consideration of how decisions in one area of school life were likely to affect other aspects. Many commented on the timespan needed for staff to review and develop each subject thoroughly and agree on a way forward:

> If you are going to do it properly it takes a year to find the time for all the staff to get together on a sufficient number of occasions. To even set your aims and objectives takes a long time and when you've done that you are evaluating what should be expected at each level, what resources we have got and what we should go for. It takes a long time and I find that frustrating because while we're spending careful time on that I can see in the background a lot of other things piling up.

The need to review and implement each subject as the initial and revised orders became available and the concern to produce policies and plans for the curriculum and other areas, which has heightened with the prospect of OFSTED inspections, has rendered impossible whole school involvement in all policy initiatives.

In larger schools, in order to respond more quickly to the need for change, small teams of staff worked on curriculum areas simultaneously. For example, in one primary school with 17 teachers in addition to the head, staff had the choice of joining working parties on music, art or PE in order to develop policy documents for those subjects and to organize INSET days. They reported back to colleagues on their progress periodically in staff meetings. When their tasks were completed, they would disband and members would regroup to tackle other issues. However, while such an approach may ensure that the necessary documentation is in place, there is a danger that it may only be fully reflected in the practice of the staff who have been involved in its development. As one mathematics coordinator observed:

> We don't have a maths policy because we haven't had time as a staff to write it and the one thing I'm quite sure about is that, if the staff as a whole doesn't write it, they won't own it, they won't take any notice of it, they'll just carry on doing their own thing. We've had INSET days where people have said 'That was good, we've enjoyed

that', and we've got a lot of new equipment in school but still wherever you go you'll find people who are frightened by maths and teaching to a textbook. This fear of maths, I don't know how we overcome it.

Despite the general recognition of the importance of staff involvement in policy making, for it to have any impact on practice, perceptions of the requirements of OFSTED inspectors were leading to schools seeking to acquire a wide range of policy documents as quickly as possible. A few were considering purchasing policies produced by their LEA or private consultants, but most heads looked to other schools. One described how he had set up a support network within the LEA of headteachers that were 'good sharers'. He circulated a form to them on which to enter the policies that they had developed and were willing to exchange. Following the circulation of this information heads were able to send for each other's documents and ensure that they had a full range of policies. The modification of each of these by coordinators to tailor them to the needs of individual schools and their subsequent implementation would gradually be achieved.

Increasingly the cooperation of schools in clusters is enabling documentation to be produced cooperatively, increasing access to subject expertise and resources and providing additional opportunities for in-service training (Galton *et al.* 1991). This cooperation is especially important for small schools where the lack of staff exacerbate problems of planning for the National Curriculum and writing policy documents (see Vulliamy and Webb 1995). Among the schools visited in the second phase of the research we found a general increase in the scope and nature of cluster activities. For example, one headteacher explained how the headteachers in the cluster to which her school belonged had met with an LEA adviser for a session on school development planning, the teachers in her school were combining with one cluster school for 'twilight' in-service on mathematics and another to develop a school asssessment portfolio, three teachers from cluster schools were about to have an afternoon together to begin to develop an RE policy for the cluster and the infant teachers throughout the cluster had formed an early years group. Galton (1993: 32) suggests that in order to meet the requirements of the ERA

> there are sound arguments for clusters developing their own joint planning structures and supporting these development plans by establishing common staffing policies whereby a range of curriculum specialisms are covered by the cluster itself.

He proposes that the current largely informal clustering arrangements are taken several steps further involving the formation of 'federations' or 'consortia' whereby in turn the heads of schools within the federation assume the leadership role for an agreed period of time. However, while the headteachers in our sample welcomed the further strengthening of school links within the cluster and an increase in cluster activities, they did not wish to set up overarching management structures which would reduce the autonomy or threaten the distinctive character of their schools.

Hargreaves (1994: 64) considers that in order for organizations to be able to cope with the frenetic pace of change and decision making in the current postmodern society they need to be 'characterized by networks, alliances, tasks and projects, rather than by relatively stable roles and responsibilities which are assigned by function and department, and regulated through hierarchical supervision'. Drawing on the work of Toffler (1990), he suggests 'the moving mosaic' as an appropriate flexible and dynamic model of organization for schools which, because it encourages the sharing of expertise, the collaborative seeking for solutions and gives most teachers a turn at leading, can both empower teachers and enable schools to respond to the changing educational needs of their pupils. We found some evidence of moves towards this model within the sample schools. As demonstrated above, various groups were formed within clusters of small schools for the purpose of tackling a variety of projects. Also, as discussed in Chapter 3, the flexibility of small schools created by their non-hierarchical staffing structure enabled them readily to experiment with approaches to implementing the National Curriculum, especially subject specialist teaching. In larger schools there were examples of working parties, where members worked together on specific tasks and when these were accomplished regrouped. However, as pointed out by Hargreaves (1994: 67–8, 69), in such contexts there is a danger that 'moving mosaics' may serve to exclude colleagues as

> management teams can collaborate without their ordinary colleagues, the innovating in-group of teachers without their more skeptical counterparts, teaching staff without support staff, or members of the school without parents in the community.
> . . . the moving mosaic can easily become the manipulative mosaic, with teachers and schools having responsibility without power as the center retains control over the essentials of curriculum and testing, over the basic products which teachers must turn out.

It was certainly the case in our research that almost all the collaborative endeavour was to meet the overwhelming demands of government directives and very little was initiated solely by the perceived needs of the schools and their pupils. However, according to the values and priorities of the schools, while some of the tasks on which teachers were working were regarded merely as fulfilling a legal necessity others, although externally driven, generated considerable enthusiasm and commitment.

Management structures

The externally imposed changes introduced by the ERA and subsequent legislation have pressurized heads to innovate on all fronts speedily and continually. They have had to keep abreast of and to cope with, as one put it, 'a deluge of directives' from central government and to present these to staff as able to be accommodated within, or capable of building upon, existing school ideologies and practices. To avoid becoming overwhelmed by these multiple innovations (Wallace 1992) and in order to manage and to exert control over them, headteachers have tended to adapt or develop the management structures of their schools. As described in previous chapters, this usually involved the delegation of responsibilities to deputy heads and to curriculum coordinators.

The reflections by seven primary headteachers on their experiences (Mortimore and Mortimore 1991) demonstrate how, like the heads in our sample, they had been 'guided, to a greater or lesser extent, by what they hold to be their philosophies shaped over many years and by a number of influences' (p. 123). This leads Mortimore and Mortimore to conclude that 'the importance of having a personal philosophy cannot be overstated' and that such philosophies provide 'a raft of support' in the current tide of externally imposed changes (1991: 124). Policies, whoever produces them, tend to be viewed by those outside the school as derived from the head. Also, headteachers are accountable for school policies and in order for them to be implemented their full support is necessary. Therefore, it may be extremely difficult, if not impossible, to avoid situations where individuals and groups renegotiate initiatives and redraft documents until they arrive at what is in the mind of the head. At best such a process can be characterized as negotiation to reach a compromise acceptable by all, or at worst as delegation which is little more than benevolent manipulation. The tension between collective responsibility and clear leadership by heads, who have a vision which they believe must shape school policy and practice, is well illustrated in the following comment from one headteacher:

> What tends to be delegated is the curriculum, but the difficulty is that everyone is at a different stage in respect of how they can cope with what is delegated to them. So you can delegate certain things and your involvement, you know, is going to be fairly minimal, but some of them are going to need more help than others and the problem then is you're in a constant sort of problem in respect to time management and you wonder why you bother delegating in

the first place. For instance, I had a member of staff doing a policy document last week and she worked extremely hard on it and then she gave it to me. I took it away, went through it and the problem was, it really was not up to scratch. I could have sat down and rewritten it in an evening at home and it would have been 'right' in inverted commas, but if one is trying to be a conscientious head and is concerned about staff development then that's no good for that member of staff and so I had then to spend three evenings sitting with her up to six o'clock going through what she had done. I mean I had to almost redo it myself anyway, but not actually let her see what I had redone, but to bring what I had done as a series of suggestions. I had to do it in my own mind so that I knew what I was talking about to her and then we had to organize my suggestions into this document so that I still felt she felt her work was valued but she recognized it needed much more in it than was there already. Now that I suppose is delegation at its worst or best, depending on your point of view. It's delegation at its best, if you've got plenty of time, because she's learnt a lot through that and she'll be a better curriculum coordinator for it, but it's the time I had to spend with her which is then another chunk out of my time.

This tension is exacerbated by the timescales in which changes need to be achieved and the pressure on teachers' time.

Increasingly, in medium size schools, while the deputy was the head's main assistant, there was a move towards the creation of senior management teams, which included the deputy and the one or two teachers on A allowances or, in larger schools, B allowances. Generally, coordinators (on permanent or temporary allowances or without allowances) worked in cooperation with the head and/or deputy to develop ideas, formulate policies and draft documents which would be presented at staff meetings and modified in the light of staff feedback. These management structures were still essentially variants of the traditional two-tier model of primary school management because coordinators worked with and through the senior management team rather than assume an additional recognizable management layer. This was partly because the size of the schools meant that heads and their deputies/senior management teams could exert direct control over the work of coordinators and partly because of the problem of creating a management layer of coordinators that are differentially rewarded, often for doing what is essentially the same work.

The larger schools because they had more teachers had the greatest scope for experimenting with alternative ways of sharing out both the new responsibilities created by the ERA and those traditionally carried out by the head. In these schools the trend was to create senior management teams consisting of the head, deputy or deputies, and key stage, phase or year coordinators. In a very few schools there existed what Alexander (1992: 109) characterized as 'a management matrix' whereby:

> year leadership became a post of some importance, counterbalancing the cross-school role of curriculum leader, and introducing potential tensions over who was responsible for what. These were resolved by the formal recognition that the structure was no longer one of layers or levels, but a curriculum/year group matrix, requiring close collaboration between the parties and the involvement of all of them in policy decisions.

In the largest primary and junior schools the year leaders or the curriculum coordinators (other than for the core subjects), who were on B allowances, formed a managerial layer in a three-tier management structure which, while it made policy formulation speedier and more streamlined, reduced the influence of classteachers over decisions on whole school issues (a trend which Ball [1994] has documented in secondary schools). For example, one head of a large junior school had set up a staffing structure which enabled him to delegate curriculum, financial and administrative responsibilities and therefore create the opportunity to maintain an overview of all aspects of the life of the school. He explained why the school had come to appoint two deputies in autumn 1992 – one for LMS and one to coordinate the curriculum:

> I found with being a devolved school and with the growing issues relating to National Curriculum and having to spend an inordinate amount of time planning, thinking, reading, revising, discussing with curriculum leaders, discussing with year teams, discussing with the whole school, that my role as headteacher was growing out of all proportion. I didn't mind; it was exciting but the role was growing and growing and I found that with the best will in the world, even though I was working 25 hours a day and becoming a lodger at home, initiatives from staff, initiatives from parents were becoming held back because I wasn't able to deal with them in the timescale that I should to keep interest and motivation going.

He described how he tried to meet briefly with his deputies each day in order that the three of them could update each other and that frequently they had planning days to work together on priority issues. Once a week the three of them met the four year coordinators and the year coordinators met with the teachers in their year group, often during the time provided by a long assembly taken by the head. While sometimes there was 'meeting overload' on weeks where there was also a whole staff meeting, the communication of information across the school was thought to be improving, especially since all the meetings had become minuted and so there was a record of what had been discussed and agreed. The head felt that the structure was working well because quality work was being accomplished much more speedily.

Another large primary school was also run by a senior management team consisting of the headteacher, two deputies, who were also phase coordinators, and the two other phase leaders. The head took overall responsibility for the budget and financial issues and staffing in relation to deployment and career development. One deputy was responsible for staff INSET and initial training and the other for curriculum and assessment. The head explained:

> One of the philosophies I'm looking at is the idea of local management where you put the decision making down to the nearest base where it actually happens. So if you're developing the curriculum you put it down to the staff who are going to be closely involved with it, rather than beaver away at a policy statement and simply say 'this is what you do' . . . So it's trying to move decision making down, but you have to have people to coordinate it and pull it together.

The head stressed how important it was that the deputy responsible for curriculum development should have the freedom to make decisions and to push developments forward in the ways that he considered best, providing that he operated within the agreed framework of school aims and preferred teaching approaches. As he had a class and interacted daily with pupils and teachers in relation to the curriculum, the head considered that he was in the best position to judge what needed to be done. The head also recognized that, if coordinators had to continually seek his approval for decisions, as discovered by the junior school head quoted above, a bottleneck would develop at the top and he would become overburdened with work.

School development plans

Advocates of school development plans (for example, Hargreaves and Hopkins 1991) argue that these are a vehicle for bringing together national and local policies and the aims and development needs of individual schools and in so doing enabling schools to manage and control change and to give staff ownership of that change and create a shared sense of direction. If tackled with thoroughness, then, as detailed by Southworth (1993), school development planning is a complex and time consuming process. He considers that it requires:

> policies be discussed and agreed; implementation plans be produced and resourced; INSET opportunities be integrated with the plans;

school and classroom organisational arrangements be reviewed and adjustments made; parents and governors be informed and involved; pupils' views and reactions be noted and monitored; unexpected developments and mandates be dealt with; allowances be made for personnel changes; the emotional reactions to the change and the change process be dealt with; and the whole enterprise be kept under review and the validity of the original plan considered from time to time.

(pp.80–1)

In discussing their school development plans some heads described them as derived from and inseparable from LMS:

We have had a school development plan now for four years as we were a pilot LMS school and the moment you become involved in LMS you must have a plan, as you cannot have money without a plan to spend it, so LMS and school development plans came together. Before that there was little point in having one because you couldn't deliver it if the people concerned didn't give you the money. The most important aspect of the plan from my point of view is to increase the physical size of the school because to deliver the National Curriculum effectively we need more space and more teachers – the space first and then the teachers.

However, because LMS was phased in in stages most heads' initial experience of school development plans was that they dealt solely or predominantly with curriculum issues and associated staff development. Plans only became extended to other areas as and when their schools received fully delegated budgets. As pointed out in the above quotation, there was little point in drawing up other than very tentative plans for areas over which you had little or no control.

While development plans contributed to a controlled approach to change, they appeared as yet to have made minimal contribution to staff or governor ownership of that change. As found by Osborn and Black (1994), the rhetoric of collaborative school development planning proved problematic in practice. In several schools headteachers admitted that they had written the current school development plans themselves or in consultation with their senior management teams:

Now each head does a management plan – well, they say the school does a management plan and the head with the governors does a management plan but in practical terms I can't get the governors together and I'm very conscious of the staff having lots of other constraints. I think 99 per cent of heads actually take it home and sit down and do it. That's a shame because it's supposed to be a whole school policy document but you can't. There isn't time.

In schools where development plans were a cooperative venture, they tended to be derived from staff brainstorming as to what should be incorporated and/or discussion of drafts usually on a staff training day convened for that purpose. However, staff were much more likely to be involved in curriculum related planning than in other areas.

Continual changes to the National Curriculum orders had undermined the usefulness of school development plans because heads had had to make numerous alterations to their long term curriculum goals, the INSET and resources necessary to support these and the timescales for achieving them. Also, because of the amount and pace of change, school development plans were driven almost entirely by the government's agenda and school priorities identified before the ERA 'were pushed on the back burner'. Notwithstanding the problems of devising plans that were sufficiently flexible to allow for their continuous adaptation and of creating opportunities to involve staff and governors in their creation, about a third of the headteachers referred spontaneously to the role of development planning in achieving change, especially curriculum change. School development plans were becoming increasingly valued for clarifying and listing priorities, target setting, deciding on strategies for managing the necessary changes and identifying criteria to evaluate how far targets had been achieved. Plans were gradually becoming more detailed and incorporating anticipated national initiatives, space to revise that which was already in place in response to changes in the orders and schools' individual priorities.

Increasingly heads considered that through more systematic and considered planning they were able to tie together school needs, resourcing and staff INSET and in some cases were also able to link salary incentive points with specific initiatives. As one deputy head explained:

> RE has staggered on for years and years and nothing really has been done, so to try and force things with the support of the agreed LEA syllabus the coordinator has an incentive point for a year to do RE, which so far she is making a good job of. While RE appears in the management plan we [the senior management team] wanted it tighter than that, so I then did a sheet which gives the initiative, the 12-month timescale and the three targets. I met with the coordinator to agree on the targets and we agreed on the criteria for deciding whether the targets had been achieved or not. Then she filled in the rest of the sheet about what resources do you think that you might want and what is to be done within the three targets and that's all there on the sheet. It will be the basis for the review and then we can

decide if that's the end of it, and if so, what is the watching brief on RE.

The deputy stressed that the notion of 'a watching brief' was an important one because schools were in danger of pursuing one initiative after another without building in mechanisms to ensure improvements were maintained. Such examples of where staff roles and appraisal and specific tasks and task evaluation were incorporated into school development plans demonstrated their likely future potential in the creation and management of change.

Quality assurance mechanisms

Murgatroyd and Morgan (1992: 45) describe quality assurance as 'the determination of standards, appropriate methods and quality require-ments by an expert body, accompanied by a process of inspection or evaluation that examines the extent to which practice meets these standards'. While the general thrust of the current growth in managerial-ism – for example, document production and systems for target setting – is that it should lead to greater quality and higher standards in education, the introduction of agreement trialing in relation to National Curriculum assessment and OFSTED inspections are two mechanisms which are specifically and explicitly concerned with quality assurance.

As discussed in Chapter 1, the voluntary national pilot of the KS2 tests in the core subjects was disrupted by teacher action. Where tests were carried out they were marked by teachers in line with mark sheets and there was no requirement for external checking. While teachers at KS2 participated in the selection or design of pupil National Curriculum attainment records and the development of Teacher Assessment (TA) in their schools, especially in relation to planning for assessment and the compilation of individual pupil portfolios, they received little or no assessment training other than that provided by KS1 colleagues and assessment coordinators. Early on in the introduction of the National Curriculum LEAs introduced the notion of agreement trials at KS1 to bring together teachers from different schools to explore judgements on pupil performance and trained moderators to visit schools and audit TA levels in accordance with the SEAC's (1991) requirements. However, there were no audit moderation arrangements for TA at KS2, although in 1994 the SCAA appointed two agencies to pilot approaches to quality assurance in assessment based on school clusters and visiting moderators. James (1994) highlights the kinds of problems KS1 teachers experienced in carrying out TA and providing evidence to support their judgements. These problems suggest that, without LEA training and support, school agreement trials and the school portfolios based on them may make only a limited contribution to standardizing assessments. However, Clarke and Christie (1995), who observed the practice of agreement trialing evolve across 22 schools over a three-year period, found that the practice was occurring with increased frequency because it was valued by teachers and that it served a school improvement function. They concluded that this was not because agreement trialing determines a consistent interpretation of the National Curriculum performance levels but rather because of its potential for collaborative learning and the fact that it 'is one of the few situations where legitimised teacher time in meetings actually considers the primary functions of teaching and learning' (p. 11).

OFSTED (1994b: 8) prescribes that headteachers should be: 'monitoring the work undertaken in classes to see how the work planned and prepared is actually transacted and assessed'; and 'evaluating the teaching techniques and organisational strategies employed'. Consequently headteachers viewed the more direct monitoring of the implementation of plans and policies in practice, which would involve formal classroom observation, as likely to become an increasingly important aspect of their role and in some cases of their deputy headteachers and of coordinators in relation to their subjects. As portrayed in Southworth's (1995) study of Ron Lacey, headteachers have always sought to control quality through monitoring what occurred in school by means such as conversations with staff and children, 'tours' of the school, informal feedback from staff and 'showing assemblies' where children's work is displayed. Whereas Ron Lacey judged what he saw against his own criteria of what constituted quality, the headteachers in our sample were also applying the criteria in the OFSTED (1993b) handbook for inspections.

Generally coordinators, while wanting opportunities to visit colleagues' classrooms to find out what was happening, were uncomfortable with the notion of observing for monitoring purposes. Humphreys (1994: 186), describing his experience as an OFSTED inspector helping five schools for primary age children to self-inspect, encountered 'the most remarkable set of avoidance tactics to evade observation of classroom practice'. He attributes this in part to a school culture where teachers are unaccustomed to discussing practice on the basis of evidence and where professional criticism was likely to be taken personally. He also cites lack of understanding of the OFSTED criteria, on which they were to base their judgements, as another reason for the possibility of observation inducing excuses and in some cases even panic. Increasingly in the schools in our sample, headteachers were encouraging staff to become familiar with those parts of the OFSTED handbook relevant to their responsibilities and to introduce the language and concepts used into staff discussion during meetings and school-based INSET. This was viewed as a necessary part of OFSTED preparation rather than a means of enriching or focusing the discourse. As observed by Southworth and

Fielding (1994), who raise a number of concerns about the potential of inspections to contribute to school improvement, while the main thrust of inspections is what goes on inside classrooms, the OFSTED handbook offers a rather straightforward and unproblematic view of teaching and learning.

Preparation for possible OFSTED inspections focused attention on the need for teachers to become familiar not only with the criteria for inspection set out in *The Handbook for the Inspection of Schools* (OFSTED 1993b) but also with the experience of being observed. The power of the inspectors and the corresponding powerlessness of the teachers, who were to be passive recipients of the judgements made upon them, made the prospect of being inspected especially threatening and something to which heads wanted teachers to become adjusted well in advance. Headteachers were concerned about likely teacher stress induced by the inspection process itself and the impact of any negative findings on governors and parents. Thorough preparations were generally viewed as essential in order to reduce apprehension and to give teachers the confidence to respond to the inspection as naturally as possible. Once OFSTED inspections are established and if the revised framework and guidance for inspections is both more focused and appropriate for primary schools, current levels of anxiety generated by the prospect of inspections will hopefully be a passing phenomenon. In the meantime, it is very questionable whether such fear-induced monitoring based on external criteria can bring about any changes of fundamental benefit to schools.

Many headteachers expressed the need for training in classroom observation as they were unsure exactly what they were looking for, how to look for it and how to record their observations and judgements. Headteachers had experience of observing in relation to teacher appraisal. However, the Leverhulme Teacher Appraisal project (Wragg *et al*. 1994) raised questions about the quality of the classroom observations carried out and therefore their potential to improve classroom practice:

> Despite the requirement that teachers should be observed twice, some 28% were only seen once. About half the observations lasted under 45 minutes per occasion, and three teachers claimed they had been observed for less than ten minutes.
>
> (Wragg *et al*. 1994: 12)

Lack of appropriate skills and time to observe are extremely important constraints on the potential of monitoring to contribute to the understanding and subsequent development of classroom practice.

Whole school collaboration: a shifting terrain?

The 1980s emphasis upon the virtues of collegiality contained strong undercurrents of the promotion of more democratic approaches to the management of primary schools. As suggested by Southworth (1987: 67) 'the idealized "collegial school" has small working groups of teachers feeding back suggestions for school-wide changes to the collectivity of the whole staff meeting for decision-making'. However, Campbell and Southworth (1992) point out that the advocacy of collegiality is made more on the basis of prescription than on research-based studies of school practice. Such prescriptions both fail adequately to define what is meant by collegiality and fail to recognize the obstacles to its successful achievement. Thus, for example, ethnographic accounts of primary school cultures reveal the extent to which traditional cultural patterns must alter to accommodate more collegial styles of working (Nias *et al.* 1989). Examples of such traditional cultural patterns include the individualist culture of teaching (Acker 1991) and the formidable concentration of power in headteachers (Southworth 1995).

As indicated in the introduction to this chapter, exhortations for further collaborative management in primary schools have continued to be made in the post-ERA context by policy makers and educationalists. However, where terms such as 'collegiality', 'collaboration', 'teamwork' and 'whole school approaches' are often used interchangeably, especially in management manuals (see for example, Harrison and Gill 1992), our analysis suggests that there have been subtle shifts in the meaning of such terms or descriptors and in their realization in practice in the pre- and post-ERA context. The beginnings of such changes are signposted in Nias *et al.*'s (1992) comparison of the findings from ethnographic case studies of whole school curriculum development in the early stages of the implementation of the ERA with their pre-ERA research into cultures of collaboration. Nias *et al.* (1989: 247) state:

> We believe it is necessary to draw a distinction between 'whole schools' and collegial ones. In 'whole schools' it appears to be acceptable to both the heads and the teachers that the head plays a powerful and pivotal role. By contrast, in collegial schools, because such a role conception for the head is regarded as a barrier to collegiality (Campbell 1985), the head would act differently. Moreover, in 'whole schools' there is a high degree of consultation but, given the head's role, this should not be mistaken for teacher democracy.

The extent to which some current notions of 'collaboration' can be premised on a top-down dictatorial approach rather than a democratic collegial one is indicated by the Audit Commission's view of 'collaborative management':

> Although final decisions on a school's development plan rest with the governing body, the Headteacher will take the lead in the preparation of the plan. The Headteacher should involve all the staff who will implement it, in order to maximise their commitment to its success.
>
> (1991:20)

As Ball notes:

> Here School Development Planning (SDPing) in effect replaces teacher planning with governor/headteacher planning. Teacher participation relates not to involvement for its own sake, as a collegial, professional or democratic concern, but for the purposes of the management of motivation. The SDP signifies and celebrates the exclusion and subjection of the teacher. Not only does the teacher lose control over classroom planning decisions, but will be monitored, judged and compared by criteria set elsewhere.
>
> (1994:61)

A useful way of characterizing our research findings is in terms of a growing tension between collegial and top-down managerial approaches to whole school change. Thus, in all the schools in the sample teachers reported varying degrees of increased cooperation with colleagues and described the contexts and ways in which they were working together. A number of factors can be seen to be combining to break down the private individualist culture of primary schools and replace it with one characterized by openness, trust and cooperation:

- joint planning and policy making in relation to National Curriculum implementation;
- working together on tasks during school closure days;
- acceptance of the wider role of curriculum coordinators by colleagues;
- the growth in school-based INSET;
- the erosion of classroom barriers by the process of appraisal;
- the emphasis on teamwork by OFSTED.

Consequently cooperative working was being extended to a range of initiatives, such as compiling school assessment portfolios, formulating school development plans, the introduction of the new code of practice for SEN and preparations for OFSTED inspections.

However, equally strong if not stronger forces appeared to be combining to promote directive management styles by headteachers, which undermine the feasibility and credibility of teachers working together collegially to formulate policies and promote continuity of practice:

- the requirement that headteachers should have clear visions of how their schools should develop and towards which staff should work;
- the importance of overt leadership by the headteacher in all aspects of the life of the school;
- headteachers' increased accountability to governors and parents;
- the pressures created by preparations for OFSTED inspections;
- requirements for greater monitoring and evaluation in the pursuit of quality assurance;
- the nature, amount and pace of externally imposed change.

As portrayed by Nias *et al.* (1992), headteachers sought to promote shared ideals and common practices through making their expectations explicit, appointing likeminded staff, inducting new staff into school practices and the use of strategies and events such as assemblies and whole school topics. The greater staff understanding of, and support for, heads' visions and willingness to translate these into policies and practice, the more heads were able, if they wished, to relinquish control and work in more collegial ways. Conversely, the more diverse the views held by staff and the greater deviation from the heads' philosophy and preferred teaching methods, the more heads were forced into a directive controlling role. Although headteachers were being pressurized into increased delegation in order to share the workload generated by the amount and pace of change, many felt the need to maintain close control over delegated tasks. Managerial structures then served to ensure that all initiatives, major or trivial, received approval before implementation. In order to enable decisions to be made and changes implemented quickly, individual coordinators or working parties were given the responsibility for developing policies and reporting back to heads and/or senior management teams. Often this involved much time and benevolent manipulation on the part of heads who took teachers through the process of task completion in such a way that the end product was congruent with the head's vision but all those involved could be satisfied with the outcome.

While there are sociological accounts of individual headteachers' determination to cling on to collaborative decision making procedures (see for example, Acker 1990b; Riseborough 1993), Pollard *et al.* (1994) in their findings from the PACE project report that between 1990 and 1992 'schools shifted from an approach to managing change that placed strong emphasis on collegial and participatory approaches towards placing more emphasis on managerial and directive approaches' (p. 75). Our evidence reported here suggests that, in all but the smallest primary schools, the impact of more recent government initiatives is taking schools further down that path. Headteachers are expected to have 'a vision of what their schools should become' which 'they will seek to establish' (Alexander *et al*. 1992: 47). They have to justify and promote this vision to parents and be held accountable for its translation into practice during their appraisal and the inspection process. The current climate thus encourages headteachers to be powerful and, if necessary, manipulative leaders in order to ensure that policies and practices agreed upon are ones that they can wholeheartedly support and defend. Furthermore, increasing job insecurity as a result of LMS in a context of rises in teachers' salaries and budget cuts places a heavy pressure on teachers to conform to headteachers' wishes and to meet the targets set for them.

In the schools in our sample, management teams were being set up which consisted of between three and six people depending on the size of school and the degree of compatibility between the head's philosophy and that of the senior teachers. Thus many initiatives and decisions tended to emanate from the hierarchy or from small groups of staff led by coordinators. Consequently this method of accomplishing change tended to distance classteachers from participation in decision making at a whole school level and further eroded their autonomy – already considerably undermined by the introduction of the National Curriculum. Increasingly, heads and senior management teams were maintaining control through mechanisms for the management of quality – for example, through school-initiated contracts linking allowances to objectives within the school development plan to be completed according to set criteria within specified timescales. While such mechanisms contributed to efficiency by clarifying expectations and creating senior management support and resources for the work to be done, they operated in opposition to attempts to create a school ethos of mutual trust and commitment where teachers work together without coercion. Anxiety over how far school policy and practice matched up to OFSTED inspection criteria was leading headteachers to operate as resident inspectors in order to monitor the classroom performance of their teachers. The reasons for such monitoring were shared with teachers and it also appeared to be being carried out with sensitivity to teachers' feelings. In addition, there was a sense – as in the early days of National Curriculum implementation – of staffs uniting in the face of adversity. However, such monitoring did generate anxiety and uncertainty among teachers which also undermined efforts to promote trust, openness and cooperation.

Conclusion

The chapters in this book portray the wide-ranging and complex interweave of demands made by the government reforms which have brought pressure to bear upon every aspect of teachers' work, both inside and outside of the classroom. Much of the thrust of the ERA, especially the implementation of the National Curriculum and testing and the policing of the system since 1994 through OFSTED, is towards uniformity and conformity, thus reducing teacher and school autonomy. Therefore, perhaps it is surprising that the most striking and lasting impression conveyed by the research was that, although at any point in the fieldwork teachers' concerns were shared and schools were addressing similar tasks resulting from the reforms, there was a tremendous diversity of response.

Several factors can be offered to account for this. It is partly inherent in the process of making and disseminating policies. Bowe *et al.*'s (1992: 120) study of the implementation of the National Curriculum in four secondary schools leads them to suggest that:

> As policy the National Curriculum remains both the object and subject of struggles over meaning. It is not so much being 'implemented' in schools as being 're-created', not so much 'reproduced' as 'produced'.

The National Curriculum orders were being interpreted and 'recreated' at all levels of decision making, at national level, for example, by the NCC, SCAA and OFSTED, at local level through the advice offered by LEAs and curriculum consultants, at school level by headteachers, senior management teams and working parties and at classroom level by classteachers. Even within the same level of policy making, interpretations contained varying and sometimes conflicting messages. Hence, in the NCC's non-statutory guidance and publications in the Curriculum Guidance series, which supported the introduction of the initial orders, primary teachers could find much support for subject integration and 'progressive' teaching methods. This guidance became increasingly at variance with the pronouncements of politicians and OFSTED. Such contradictions at the national level of policy making confuse the situation but, in so doing, serve to make space for and to legitimate alternative interpretations of legislation at LEA and school level.

At school level when and how the reforms are introduced into schools and the priority that various aspects of these are given are largely dependent upon headteachers, who act as the gatekeepers for all new information. As shown in the snapshots of schools presented in this book, the sample schools had very different cultures, staffing structures and ways of working and so tackled the management of change differently. Also, the progress, effect and direction that the reforms took in these schools were largely determined by the degree to which they were congruent with existing values and practices. This determined whether the reforms were perceived by headteachers as detrimental to 'the way we do things here' or regarded as a move forward. In addition, as suggested by Bowe *et al.* (1992), schools' 'innovation histories' – meaning their capacity to cope with new initiatives and past experience of managing change – had a considerable effect on reactions to the changes and how they were adapted to meet school needs.

Through some research on a global education project (Vulliamy and Webb 1993) we were able to examine the initial impact of the introduction of the National Curriculum on individual teachers. We found that teachers reacted to the new initiatives in relation both to global education and the National Curriculum according to their prior beliefs and experiences, adopting those which were consonant with their existing practices and largely ignoring those which were not. We also suggested that 'teachers' abilities creatively to interpret and to resist policy directives, as indicated in our data, should not be underestimated' (1993: 22) – a view reinforced by Woods' (1995) study of creative primary teachers. Osborn and Broadfoot (1992) characterized KS1 teachers' responses to the National Curriculum and its assessment from the PACE project in a four-fold way: cooperation, retreatism, resistance, and incorporation. Most of the teachers in their research appeared to be 'incorporating' – that is, 'feeling that they will accept the changes, but will not allow anything considered really important to be lost' (1992: 148). There are certainly many examples of incorporation in our data – for example, teachers deviating from their plans in order to hold on to the role of opportunism and spontaneity in responding to children's interests in their teaching. However, there are also examples of the introduction of the National Curriculum being used by individuals both to develop their practice, for example in relation to differentiation, and to experiment with new approaches, such as cooperative groupwork in science. In some aspects of practice – for example, the move by schools towards more separate subject teaching – working in new ways has led to beliefs and assumptions being questioned and to a change in attitudes. In other areas, especially in relation to recording National Curriculum attainment, teachers have seen their worst fears realized. Owing to the hard work and imaginative interpretation of the National Curriculum by many teachers, gains have been made in classroom practice through its introduction. However, if time for reflection and energy for innovation had not been swallowed up by excessive paperwork, which often made little or no contribution to teaching and learning, much more could have been achieved.

In relation to new managerial roles, where there were considerable practical barriers to change but fundamental beliefs were not threatened, many teachers tackled new areas of work with considerable commitment. For example, some curriculum coordinators derived a great deal of satisfaction from contributing to the professional development of colleagues through the provision of ideas and INSET. The majority of deputy headteachers welcomed their role as assistant headteacher and their increased power as leaders, especially in relation to the curriculum. As concluded in the previous chapter, for some headteachers the reforms opened up new opportunities for school improvement and their own professional development.

As Woods (1995: 176) reveals, the changes 'have been cathartic for some teachers' sense of self' leading them to question all aspects of the values, knowledge and experiences underpinning their teaching. Insecurity, stress and overwork have taken a heavy toll on some teachers, often the most conscientious and committed teachers, heads argued. However, many have come through the last five years clearer about their educational beliefs, recognizing what is worth fighting for in primary education and what needs to change, more politically aware of how to go about this at the micro and macro level and possessing more self-confidence and communication skills.

Schools are being encouraged to embrace collegial management styles and are being assessed on the quality of their teamwork. Consequently, in-service training for heads, senior management and coordinators tends to reproduce the accepted rhetoric of the 1980s rather than address the reality of school management in the 1990s which is needed in order to help schools to understand the dilemmas of their position, the choices open to them and the likely resulting consequences. As we have shown here, the origins and nature of the reforms together with the pace at which they had to be implemented is resulting in the institutionalization of increasingly directive and controlling mechanisms. Also, although greater sharing and cooperation were acknowledged as initial unanticipated benefits of the introduction of the National Curriculum, in the sample schools teachers were increasingly questioning the rationale and efficiency of whole school meetings and the value of spending time in this way. The tensions generated by trying to create conditions for cooperative working in the context of increased managerialism were present to some extent in all schools. How these tensions were accommodated in practice varied according to factors such as school size, staff cohesion and shared institutional values, the headteacher's management style and length of time in post, and each school's prior experience of curriculum development and change. Although too early to predict the long term effects of the current growth in managerialism on the culture of primary schools, our research suggests that in the current climate it would be difficult to develop further the cooperative working provided by the initial stages of National Curriculum implementation.

It is all too easy from a position outside schools to feel pessimistic about the future of primary education. Such pessimism is readily fuelled by media derision, by OFSTED (1995) claims that in more than a quarter of lessons at KS2 pupil standards were unsatisfactory, and by the continuing underfunding of primary education, which leads to rises in class size, lack of staffing flexibility, inadequate equipment and teaching materials and the consequent stifling of innovation. The pressures on teachers are intense and the workloads excessive. Without additional resourcing, primary schools will be unable to adapt and develop further, and therefore are likely to find it increasingly difficult not only to respond to the demands created by 'the deluge of government directives' but also, and more importantly, to the educational needs of pupils in the twenty-first century. The only solutions currently offered by the government are to go backwards and reinstate whole class teaching and streaming and to police the system through inspections. The antidote to such pessimism is to go into schools and talk to and observe teachers at work, as we did in this research. Witnessing their commitment to teaching, the unceasing ideas and enthusiasm that they bring to it and their resolve to see changes in a positive light and to make these work for their pupils and schools, optimism is rekindled.

References

Achilles, C.M., Nye, B.A., Zahanas, J.B. and Fulton, B.D. (1993) 'The Lasting Benefits Study (LBS) in grades 4 and 5 (1990–1991): A legacy from Tennessee's four-year (K3) class size study (1985–1989), Project STAR', paper to North Carolina Association for Research in Education, Greensboro, NC.

Acker, S. (1990a) Managing the drama: The headteacher's work in an urban primary school, *Sociological Review*, 38 (2): 247–71.

Acker, S. (1990b) Teachers' culture in an English primary school: Continuity and change, *British Journal of Sociology of Education*, 11 (3): 257–73.

Acker, S. (1991) Teacher relationships and educational reform in England and Wales, *The Curriculum Journal*, 2 (3): 301–16.

Aldrich, R. (1988) The National Curriculum: An historical perspective. In D. Lawton and C. Chitty (eds) *The National Curriculum*, Bedford Way Paper 33. Institute of Education: University of London.

Alexander, R. (1988) Garden or jungle? Teacher development and informal primary education. In A. Blyth (ed.) *Informal Primary Education Today*. London: Falmer Press.

Alexander, R. (1992) *Policy and Practice in Primary Education*. London: Routledge.

Alexander, R. (1993) 'Innocence and experience: Reconstructing primary education', inaugural lecture, University of Leeds, 13 December.

Alexander, R. and Campbell, J. (1994) Beware Dearing's time warp, *Times Educational Supplement*, 21 January.

Alexander, R., Rose, J. and Woodhead, C. (1992) *Curriculum Organisation and Classroom Practice in Primary Schools: A Discussion Paper*. London: DES.

Andrews, K. and Jacobs, J. (1990) *Punishing the Poor: Poverty under Thatcher*. London: Macmillan.

Assistant Masters and Mistresses Association (AMMA) (1992) *Primary Education, A Contribution to the Debate*. London: AMMA.

Atkin, J., Bastiani, J. and Goode, J. (1988) *Listening to Parents: An Approach to the Improvement of Home–School Relations*. London: Croom Helm.

Audit Commission (1991) *The Management of Primary Schools*. London: Audit Commission.

Ball, S.J. (1990a) Markets, inequality and urban schooling, *Urban Review*, 22 (2): 85–100.

Ball, S.J. (1990b) A National Curriculum for the 1990s, *NUT Educational Review*, 4 (1): 9–12.

Ball, S.J. (1990c) *Politics and Policy Making in Education*. London: Routledge.

Ball, S.J. (1994) *Education Reform, A Critical and Post-structural Approach*. Buckingham: Open University Press.

Bennett, N. (1994) *Class Size in Primary Schools*. Exeter: University of Exeter School of Education.

Bennett, N. and Cass, A. (1989) The effects of group composition on group interactive processes and pupil understanding, *British Educational Research Journal*, 15 (1): 19–32.

Bennett, N., Desforges, C., Cockburn, A. and Wilkinson, B. (1984) *The Quality of Pupil Learning Experiences*. London: Lawrence Erlbaum Associates.

Bennett, N. and Dunne, E. (1992) *Managing Classroom Groups*. Hemel Hempstead: Simon and Schuster Education.

Bennett, N., Summers, M. and Askew, M. (1994) Knowledge for teaching and teaching performance. In A. Pollard (ed.) *Look Before You Leap? Research Evidence for the Curriculum at Key Stage Two*. London: Tufnell Press.

Bennett, S.N., Wragg, E.C., Carre, C.G. and Carter, D.S.G. (1992) A longitudinal study of primary teachers' perceived competence in, and concerns about, National Curriculum implementation, *Research Papers in Education*, 7 (1): 53–78.

Blease, D. and Lever, D. (1992) What do primary headteachers really do? *Educational Studies*, 18 (2): 185–99.

Bowe, R., Ball, S.J. with Gold, A. (1992) *Reforming Education and Changing Schools*. London: Routledge.

Boydell, D. (1990) '. . . The gerbil on the wheel': Conversations with primary headteachers about the implications of the ERA, *Education 3–13*, 18 (2): 20–4.

Brehony, K.J. (1990) Neither rhyme nor reason: Primary schooling and the National Curriculum. In M. Flude and M. Hammer (eds) *The Education Reform Act 1988*. London: Falmer Press.

Brown, G. and Wragg, E.C. (1993) *Questioning*. London: Routledge.

Brown, P. (1990) The 'third wave': Education and the ideology of parentocracy, *British Journal of Sociology of Education*, 11 (1): 65–85.

Burstall, C. (1992) Playing the numbers game in class, *Education Guardian*, 7 April.

Burton, L. and Weiner, G. (1990) Social justice and the National Curriculum, *Research Papers in Education*, 5 (3): 203–27.

Campbell, P. and Southworth, G. (1992) Rethinking collegiality: Teachers' views. In N. Bennett, M. Crawford and C. Riches (eds) *Managing Change in Education: Individual and Organisational Perspectives*. London: Paul Chapman.

Campbell, R.J. (1985) *Developing the Primary School Curriculum*. London: Holt, Rinehart and Winston.

Campbell, R.J. (1991) Children and subjects: A national perspective, summary of paper presented by Colin Richards. In *Papers from the Third Annual Conference of the Association for the Study of Primary Education*. ASPE.

Campbell, R. J. (1992) 'The National Curriculum in primary schools: A dream at conception, a nightmare at delivery', keynote lecture given to the British Association for the Advancement of Science Annual Conference, Southampton University, August.

Campbell, R.J. (1994) Manageability and control of the primary curriculum. In G. Southworth (ed.) *Readings in Primary School Development*. London: Falmer Press.

Campbell, R.J., Evans, L. and Neill, S.R.StJ. (1991) *Workloads, Achievement and Stress*. London: Assistant Masters and Mistresses Association.

Campbell, R.J. and Neill, S.R.StJ. (1990) *1330 Days*. London: AMMA.

Campbell, R.J. and Neill, S.R.StJ. (1992) *Teacher Time and Curriculum Manageability at Key Stage 1*. London: AMMA.

Campbell, R.J. and Neill, S.R.St.J. (1994) *Primary Teachers at Work*. London: Routledge.

Central Advisory Council for Education (England) (CACE) (1967) *Children and their Primary Schools*, (The Plowden Report). London: HMSO.

Chitty, C. (ed.) (1993) *The National Curriculum: Is It Working?* Harlow: Longman.

Clarke, K. (1991) 'Primary education – A statement', text of a statement made by the Secretary of State for Education and Science, 3 December. London: Department of Education and Science.

Clarke, P. and Christie, T. (1995) 'Trialling agreement – A discourse for a change', Centre for Formative Assessment Studies, University of Manchester mimeo.

Clegg, D. and Billington S. (1994) *Making the Most of Your Inspection*. London: Falmer Press.

Conner, C. (ed.) (1988) *Topic and Thematic Work in the Primary and Middle Years*. Cambridge: Cambridge Institute of Education.

Conner, C. (1994) Managing assessment: Have we learned any lessons from the experience of National Curriculum assessment? In G. Southworth (ed.) *Readings in Primary School Development*. London: Falmer Press.

Coulson, A.A. (1980) The role of the primary head. In T.Bush, R. Glatter and J. Goodey (eds) *Approaches to School Management*. London: Harper and Row.

Coulson, A. (1986) The managerial work of primary school headteachers, *Sheffield Papers in Education Management*, 48. Sheffield: Sheffield City Polytechnic.

Cyster, R., Clift, P.S. and Battle, S. (1979) *Parental Involvement in Primary Schools*. Slough: NFER.

Dainton, S. (1994) The National Curriculum and the policy process. London: ATL, mimeo. Forthcoming in M. Barber, S. Dainton and C. Woodhead (eds) *Keele Studies in Education Policy: The National Curriculum*. Keele: Keele University Press.

Daugherty, R. (1992) 'The future development of the primary curriculum in Wales', text of a speech to the primary advisers of Wales, 4 December. Llandrindod Wells, Powys.

Day, C., Hall, C., Gammage, P. and Coles, M. (1993) *Leadership and Curriculum in the Primary School*. London: Paul Chapman Publishing Ltd.

Day, C., Johnston, D. and Whitaker, P. (1985) *Managing Primary Schools: A Professional Development Approach*. London: Harper and Row.

Day, C., Whitaker, P. and Johnston, D. (1990) *Managing Primary Schools in the 1990s*. London: Paul Chapman Publishing Ltd.

Dean, J. (1994) *Second Survey of the Organisation of LEA Inspection and Advisory Services*. Slough: NFER.

Dean, J. (1995) *Managing the Primary School*, 2nd edn. London: Routledge.

Dearing, R. (1993a) *The National Curriculum and Its Assessment, Final Report*. London: SCAA.

Dearing, R. (1993b) *The National Curriculum and Its Assessment, An Interim Report*. London: NCC/SEAC.

DES (1975) *A Language for Life*, (The Bullock Report). London: HMSO.

DES (1978a) *Primary Education in England, A Survey by HM Inspectors of Schools*. London: HMSO.

DES (1978b) *Special Educational Needs*, (The Warnock Report). London: HMSO.

DES (1982a) *Education 5–9: An Illustrative Survey of 80 First Schools in England*. London: HMSO.

DES (1982b) *Mathematics Counts*, (The Cockroft Report). London: HMSO.

DES (1985a) *The Curriculum from 5 to 16*. London: HMSO.

DES (1985b) *Education 8 to 12 in Combined and Middle Schools, An HMI Survey*. London: HMSO.

DES (1989a) *National Curriculum: From Policy to Practice*. London: DES.

DES (1989b) *The Teaching and Learning of History and Geography*. London: HMSO.

DES (1989c) *Discipline in Schools*, (The Elton Report). London: HMSO.

DES (1991a) *The Education (School Teacher Appraisal) Regulations 1991*, SI No. 1511. London: HMSO.

DES (1991b) *Statistics of Education: Schools 1991*. London: DES.

DES/Welsh Office (1977) *A New Partnership for Our Schools*, (The Taylor Report). London: HMSO.

Desforges, C. (1985) Matching tasks to children's attainments. In N. Bennett and C. Desforges (eds) *Recent Advances in Classroom Research*. Edinburgh: Scottish Academic Press.

DFE (1994) *Our Children's Education, The Updated Parents' Charter*. London: HMSO.

DHSS (1968) *Report of the Committee on Local Authorities and Allied Personal Social Services*, (The Seebohm Report). London: HMSO.

Dodds, D. (1994) Soaring like turkeys? The functioning of school governing bodies in traditional working class communities and areas of deprivation, *Education 3–13*, 22 (2): 49–52.

Edwards, A. (1993) Curriculum co-ordination: A lost opportunity for primary school development? *School Organisation*, 13 (1): 51–9.

Elliott, J. (1991) *Action Research for Educational Change*. Milton Keynes: Open University Press.

Emery, H. (1996) Children evaluating and assessing their progress in learning. In R. Webb (ed.) *Cross-curricular Primary Practice*. London: Falmer Press.

Finch, J. (1986) *Research and Policy: The Uses of Qualitative Methods in Social and Educational Research*. Lewes: Falmer Press.

Fowler, A. (1993) *Saving For Pay*. London: ATL.

Fullan, M.G. (1991) *The New Meaning of Educational Change*. London: Cassell.

Fullan, M. (1992) *Successful School Improvement*. Buckingham: Open University Press.

Fullan, M. and Hargreaves, A. (1992) *What's Worth Fighting for in your School?* Buckingham: Open University Press.

Galton, M. (1989) *Teaching in the Primary School*. London: David Fulton.

Galton, M. (1993) *Managing Education in Small Primary Schools*, ASPE Paper Number 4. London: Trentham Books Ltd.

Galton, M. (1995) *Crisis in the Primary Classroom*. London: David Fulton.

Galton, M., Fogelman, K., Hargreaves, L. and Cavendish, S. (1991) *The Rural Schools Curriculum Enhancement National Evaluation (SCENE) Project*. London: DES.

Galton, M., Simon, B. and Croll, P. (1980) *Inside the Primary Classroom*. London: Routledge and Kegan Paul.

Gipps, C. (1995) Teacher assessment and teacher development in primary schools, *Education 3–13*, 23 (1): 8–12.

Gipps, C., McCallum, B. and Brown, M.L. (1994) 'What have we learnt from national assessment at key stage one? A retrospective', British Educational Research Association conference paper, University of Oxford, September.

Glaser, B. and Strauss, A. (1967) *The Discovery of Grounded Theory*. Chicago, IL: Aldine.

Hackett, G. (1995) Woodhead castigates progressives, *Times Educational Supplement*, 27 January.

Haigh, G. (1993) Trapped by trivia? *School Management Update, Times Educational Supplement*, 29 January.

Haigh, G. (1994a) Teacher's big helper, *Times Educational Supplement*, 7 October.

Haigh, G. (1994b) Why deputies need not dog their heads, *Times Educational Supplement*, 3 June.

Handy, C. and Aitkin, R. (1986) *Understanding Schools as Organisations*. London: Penguin Books.

Hardie, B. (1991) *Marketing the Primary School: An Introduction for Teachers and Governors*. Plymouth: Northcote House.

Hargreaves, A. (1989) *Curriculum and Assessment Reform*. Milton Keynes: Open University Press.

Hargreaves, A. (1994) *Changing Teachers, Changing Times. Teachers' Work and Culture in the Postmodern Age*. London: Cassell.

Hargreaves, D.H. and Hopkins, D. (1991) *The Empowered School*. London: Cassell.

Harland, J. (1990) *The Work and Impact of Advisory Teachers*. Slough: NFER.

Harrison, M. and Gill, S. (1992) *Primary School Management*. Oxford: Heinemann.

Hastings, N. and Schwieso, J. (1994) Kindly take your seats, *Times Educational Supplement*, 21 October.

Hayes, D. (1994) A primary headteacher in search of a collaborative climate. In G. Southworth (ed.) *Readings in Primary School Development*. London: Falmer Press.

Hellawell, D. (1991) The changing role of the head in the primary school in England, *School Organisation*, 11 (3): 321–37.

Helps, R. (1993) The role of deputy head teachers in decision making, *Education Today*, 43 (4): 49–53.

Hill, T. (1989) *Managing the Primary School*. London: David Fulton.

Hofkins, D. (1994) Social worker back-up demanded, *Times Educational Supplement*, 21 October.

Holly, P. and Southworth, G. (1989) *The Developing School*. London: Falmer Press.

Horbury, A. and Pears, H (1994) Collaborative groupwork: How infant children can manage it, *Education 3–13*, 22 (3): 20–8.

House of Commons Select Committee (1986) Education, Science and Arts Committee, *Third Report: Achievement in Primary Schools*, Vol. 1. London: HMSO.

House of Commons Select Committee on Education (1994) *The Disparity in Funding between Primary and Secondary Schools*. London: HMSO.

Hughes, M., Wikeley, F. and Nash, T. (1994) *Parents and their Children's Schools*. Oxford: Basil Blackwell.

Humphreys, K. (1994) My ball, your game: Dilemmas in self-regulation according to the OFSTED criteria, *British Journal of In-service Education*, 20 (2): 181–93.

ILEA (1985) *Improving Primary Schools*, Report of the Committee on Primary Education, Chair Norman Thomas. London: ILEA.

Jackson, B. (1964) *Streaming: An Education System in Miniature*. London: Routledge and Kegan Paul.

James, M. (1993) 'Everything in moderation: Experience of quality assurance at key stage one', British Educational Research Association conference paper, Liverpool University, September.

James, M. (1994) 'Teachers' assessment and national testing in England: Roles and relationships', British Educational Research Association conference paper, University of Oxford, September.

Jenkins, C. (1994) The 'luxury' that becomes indispensable, *Times Educational Supplement*, 11 November.

Jones, G. and Hayes, D. (1991) Primary headteachers and the ERA two years on: The pace of change and its impact upon schools, *School Organisation*, 11 (2): 211–21.

Jowett, S. and Baginsky, M., with MacNeil, M. (1991) *Building Bridges: Parental Involvement in Schools*. Windsor: NFER–Nelson.

Judd, J. (1994) Teachers 'have to be social workers', *The Independent*, 21 October.

Kelly, A.V. (1990) *The National Curriculum: A Critical Review*. London: Paul Chapman Publishing Ltd.

Kelly, V. and Blenkin, G. (1993) Never mind the quality: Feel the breadth and balance. In R.J. Campbell (ed.) *Breadth and Balance in the Primary Curriculum*. London: Falmer Press.

Kerry, T. and Eggleston, J. (1988) *Topic Work in the Primary School*. London: Routledge.

Kinder, K. and Harland, J. (1991) *The Impact of INSET: The Case of Primary Science*. Slough: NFER.

Kuyser, S. (1994) Essex partnership lifts staff morale, *Times Educational Supplement*, 1 April.

Lancashire County Council (1992) *Curriculum Organisation and Classroom Practice in Primary Schools, A Response to the Above Discussion Document.* Lancashire CC.

Laws, J. and Dennison, W.F. (1991) The use of headteachers' time: leading professional or chief executive? *Education 3–13*, 19 (2): 47–57.

MacLeod, D. (1994) Schools need social workers for parents, *The Guardian*, 21 October.

Maclure, S. (1988) *Education Re-formed.* Sevenoaks: Hodder and Stoughton.

McNamara, D. (1994) *Classroom Pedagogy and Primary Practice.* London: Routledge.

Moore, J. (1992) Good planning is the key, *British Journal of Special Education*, 19 (1): 16–19.

Moore, J.L. (1992) The role of the science co-ordinator in primary schools. A survey of headteachers' views, *School Organisation*, 12 (1): 7–15.

Mortimore, P. and Mortimore, J. (eds) (1991) *The Primary Head: Roles, Responsibilities and Reflections.* London: Paul Chapman Publishing Ltd.

Mortimore, P. and Mortimore, J. (1992) *The Innovative Uses of Non-teaching Staff in Primary and Secondary Schools.* London: Institute of Education, University of London.

Mortimore, P., Sammons, P., Stoll, L., Lewis, D. and Ecob, R. (1988) *School Matters The Junior Years.* Wells: Open Books Publishing Ltd.

Murgatroyd, S. and Morgan, C. (1992) *Total Quality Management and the School.* Buckingham: Open University Press.

National Curriculum Council (1989) *A Framework for the National Curriculum, Curriculum Guidance 1.* York: NCC.

National Curriculum Council (1990a) *Education for Economic and Industrial Understanding, Curriculum Guidance 4.* York: NCC.

National Curriculum Council (1990b) *Report on Monitoring the Implementation of the National Curriculum Core Subjects 1989–1990.* York: NCC.

National Curriculum Council (1990c) *The Whole Curriculum, Curriculum Guidance 3.* York: NCC.

National Curriculum Council (1993a) *The National Curriculum at Key Stages 1 and 2, Advice to the Secretary of State for Education*, January. York: NCC.

National Curriculum Council (1993b) *Planning the National Curriculum at Key Stage 2.* York: NCC.

Nias, J. (1987) One finger, one thumb: A case study of the deputy head's part in the leadership of a nursery/infant school. In G. Southworth (ed.) *Readings in Primary School Management.* Lewes: Falmer Press.

Nias, J. (1989) *Primary Teachers Talking, A Study of Teaching as Work.* London: Routledge.

Nias, J., Southworth, G. and Campbell, P. (1992) *Whole School Curriculum Development.* London: Falmer Press.

Nias, J., Southworth, G. and Yeomans, R. (1989) *Staff Relationships in the Primary School.* London: Cassell.

NUT (1992) *Testing and Assessing 6 and 7 year Olds, The Evaluation of the 1992 Key Stage 1 National Curriculum Assessment, Final Report.* London: NUT and School of Education, University of Leeds.

Nye, B.A., Achilles, C.M., Zahanas, J.B., Fulton, B.D. and Wallenhorst,

M.P. (1992) 'Small is far better', paper to Mid–South Educational Research Association, Knoxville, TN.

OFSTED (1993a) *Curriculum Organisation and Classroom Practice in Primary Schools, A Follow-up Report.* London: HMSO.

OFSTED (1993b) *The Handbook for the Inspection of Schools.* London: HMSO.

OFSTED (1994a) *Improving Schools.* London: HMSO.

OFSTED (1994b) *Primary Matters.* London: HMSO.

OFSTED (1995) *The Annual Report of Her Majesty's Chief Inspector of Schools, Part 1.* London: HMSO.

O'Hear, P. and White, J. (1991) *A National Curriculum for All: Laying the Foundations for Success.* London: Institute for Public Policy Research.

O'Mahony, T. and Sollars, R. (1991) A professional development programme for advisory teachers, *British Journal of In-service Education*, 16 (1): 33–8.

Osborn, M. and Black, E. (1994) *Developing the National Curriculum at Key Stage 2: The Changing Nature of Teachers' Work*, report commissioned by NASUWT. Bristol: University of West of England at Bristol.

Osborn, M. and Broadfoot, P. (1992) The impact of current changes in English primary schools on teacher professionalism, *Teachers College Record*, 94 (1): 138–51.

Osborn, M. and Pollard, A. (1991) *Anxiety and Paradox: Teachers' Initial Responses to Change under the National Curriculum*, Working Paper 4, PACE Project. Bristol: Bristol Polytechnic.

Paisey, A. and Paisey, A. (1987) *Effective Management in Primary Schools.* Oxford: Basil Blackwell.

Patten, J. (1993a) Letter to Principals of Initial Teacher Training Institutions, 26 January, London: DFE.

Patten, J. (1993b) Speech to the Association of Teachers and Lecturers Conference, Cardiff, 7 April.

Pike, G. and Selby, D. (1988) *Global Teacher, Global Learner.* London: Hodder and Stoughton.

Pollard, A., Broadfoot, P., Croll, P., Osborn, M. and Abbott, D. (1994) *Changing English Primary Schools? The Impact of the Education Reform Act at Key Stage One.* London: Cassell.

Prisk, T. (1987) Letting them get on with it: A study of unsupervised group talk in an infant school. In A. Pollard (ed.) *Children and Their Primary Schools.* London: Falmer Press.

Purvis, J.R. and Dennison, W.F. (1993) Primary school deputy headship – Has ERA and LMS changed the job? *Education 3–13*, 21 (2): 15–21.

Reid, A., Forrestal, P. and Cook, J. (1989) *Small Group Learning in the Classroom.* Scarborough, Western Australia: Chalkface Press.

Reid, K., Hopkins, D. and Holly, P. (1987) *Towards the Effective School.* Oxford: Blackwell.

Reynolds J. and Saunders M. (1987) Teacher responses to curriculum policy: Beyond the 'delivery' metaphor'. In J. Calderhead (ed.) *Exploring Teachers' Thinking.* London: Cassell.

Richards, C. (1994) Four ways forward for specialists, *Times Educational Supplement*, 6 May.

Riseborough, G. (1993) Primary headship, state policy and the challenge of the

1990s: An exceptional story that disproves total hegemonic rule, *Journal of Education Policy*, 8 (2): 155–73.

SCAA (1994) *The Review of the National Curriculum, A Report on the 1994 Consultation*. London: SCAA.

SCAA (1995a) *Key Stages 1 and 2, Design and Technology, The New Requirements*. London: SCAA.

SCAA (1995b) *Planning the Curriculum at Key Stages 1 and 2*. London: SCAA.

SEAC (1991) *National Curriculum Assessment: Assessment Arrangements for Core and Other Foundation Subjects, A Moderator's Handbook 1991/92*. London: SEAC.

Shulman, L. (1986) Those who understand: Knowledge growth in teaching, *Educational Researcher*, 15 (2): 4–14.

Shulman, L. (1987) Knowledge and teaching: Foundations of the new reform, *Harvard Educational Review*, 57 (1): 1–22.

Simpson, M. (1989) *Differentiation in the Primary School: Classroom Perspectives*. Northern College Aberdeen and Dundee.

Southworth, G. (1987) Primary school headteachers and collegiality. In G. Southworth (ed.) *Readings in Primary School Management*. Lewes: Falmer Press.

Southworth, G. (1993) School leadership and school development: Reflections from research, *School Organisation*, 13 (1): 73–87.

Southworth, G. (1994) Trading places: Job rotation in a primary school. In G. Southworth (ed.) *Readings in Primary School Development*. London: Falmer Press.

Southworth, G. (1995) *Looking into Primary Headship: A Research Based Interpretation*. London: Falmer Press.

Southworth, G. and Fielding, M. (1994) School inspection for school development? In G. Southworth (ed.) *Readings in Primary School Development*. London: Falmer Press.

Spear, E. (1987) Corporate decision making versus headteacher autonomy: A question of style. In I. Craig (ed.) *Primary School Management in Action*. Harlow: Longman.

Stacey, M. (1991) *Parents and Teachers Together*. Milton Keynes: Open University Press.

Stannard, J. (1995) Managing the primary curriculum after Dearing: A rationale, *Education 3–13*, 23 (1): 3–7.

Stone, C. (1993) Questioning the new orthodoxies, *School Organisation*, 13 (2): 187–98.

Summers, M. and Kruger, C. (1994) A longitudinal study of a constructivist approach to improving primary school teachers' subject matter knowledge in science, *Teaching and Teacher Education*, 10 (5): 499–519.

Summers, M., Kruger, C. and Palacio, D. (1993) *Long-term Impact of a New Approach to Teacher Education for Primary Science: Project Report*. Oxford: Oxford University Department of Educational Studies.

Sweetman, J. (1994) Inspections in progress and in trouble, *Guardian Education*, 20 September.

Tann, C.S. (1981) Grouping and groupwork. In B. Simon and J. Willcocks (eds) *Research and Practice in the Primary Classroom*. London: Routledge and Kegan Paul.

Tann, C.S. (ed.) (1988) *Developing Topic Work in the Primary School*. London: Falmer Press.

Task Group on Assessment and Testing (TGAT) (1988) *National Curriculum, Task Group on Assessment and Testing, A Report*. London: Department of Education and Science and the Welsh Office.

Tate, N. (1994) Off the fence on common culture, *Times Educational Supplement*, 29 July.

Toffler, A. (1990) *Powershift*. New York: Bantam Books

Tricker, M. (1992) Support work in primary classrooms: Some management concerns. In G. Vulliamy and R. Webb (eds) *Teacher Research and Special Educational Needs*. London: David Fulton.

Vulliamy, G., Lewin, K. and Stephens, D. (1990) *Doing Educational Research in Developing Countries: Qualitative Strategies*. London: Falmer Press.

Vulliamy, G. and Webb, R. (1992) Analysing and validating data in teacher research. In G. Vulliamy and R. Webb (eds) *Teacher Research and Special Educational Needs*. London: David Fulton.

Vulliamy, G. and Webb, R. (1993) Progressive education and the National Curriculum: Findings from a global education research project, *Educational Review*, 45 (1): 21–41.

Vulliamy, G. and Webb, R. (1995) The implementation of the National Curriculum in small primary schools, *Educational Review*, 47 (1): 25–41.

Wallace, M. (1988) Towards a collegiate approach to curriculum management in primary and middle schools, *School Organisation*, 8 (1): 25–34.

Wallace, M. (1992) Flexible planning: A key to the management of multiple innovations. In N. Bennett, M. Crawford and C. Riches (eds) *Managing Change in Education*. London: Paul Chapman Publishing Ltd.

Waters, D. (1987) The deputy as trainee head. In I. Craig (ed.) *Primary School Management in Action*. Harlow: Longman.

Webb, R. (1989) Changing practice through consultancy-based INSET, *School Organisation*, 9 (1): 39–52.

Webb, R. (1993a) *Eating the Elephant Bit by Bit, The National Curriculum at Key Stage 2*. London: ATL.

Webb, R. (1993b) The National Curriculum and the changing nature of topic work, *The Curriculum Journal*, 4 (2): 239–51.

Webb, R. (1994) *After the Deluge: Changing Roles and Responsibilities in the Primary School*. London: ATL.

Webb, R. and Vulliamy, G. (1996) Headteachers as social workers: The hidden side of parental involvement in the primary school, *Education 3–13*, forthcoming.

West, N. (1992) *Primary Headship, Management and the Pursuit of Excellence*. Harlow: Longmans.

Weston, P. (1992) A decade for differentiation, *British Journal of Special Education*, 19 (1): 6–9.

Weston, P. (1994) Managing coherence: A letter to Sir Ron, *Education 3–13*, 22 (1): 14–23.

Whitaker, P. (1983) *The Primary Head*. London: Heinemann Educational Books.

Whitaker, P. (1993) *Managing Change in Schools*. Buckingham: Open University Press.

Winter, V. (1990) A process approach to.science. In R. Webb (ed.) *Practitioner Research in the Primary School*. London: Falmer.

Woodhead, C. (1995) *Chief Inspector's Annual Report, Commentary*. London: OFSTED.

Woods, P. (1993) *Critical Events in Teaching and Learning*. London: Falmer Press.

Woods, P. (1995) *Creative Teachers in Primary Schools*. Buckingham: Open University Press.

Woods, P. and Wenham, P. (1994) 'Politics and pedagogy: A case study in appropriation', British Educational Research Association conference paper, University of Oxford, September.

Wragg, E.C. (1993) *Primary Teaching Skills*. London: Routledge.

Wragg, E.C. and Brown, G. (1993) *Explaining*. London: Routledge.

Wragg, E.C., Wikeley, F.J., Wragg, C.M. and Haynes, G.S. (1994) 'A national survey of teacher appraisal 1992–1994', British Educational Research Association conference paper, University of Oxford, September.

Author index

Subject index

CREATIVE TEACHERS IN PRIMARY SCHOOLS

Peter Woods

Is creative teaching still possible in English schools? Can teachers maintain and promote their own interests and beliefs as well as deliver a prescribed National Curriculum?

This book explores creative teachers' attempts to pursue *their* brand of teaching despite the changes. Peter Woods has discovered a range of strategies and adaptations to this end among such teachers, including resisting change which runs counter to their own values; appropriating the National Curriculum within their own ethos; enhancing their role through the use of others; and enriching their work through the National Curriculum to provide quality learning experiences. If all else fails, such teachers remove themselves from the system and take their creativity elsewhere. A strong theme of self-determination runs through these experiences.

While acknowledging hard realities, the book is ultimately optimistic, and a tribute to the dedication and inspiration of primary teachers.

The book makes an important contribution to educational theory, showing a range of responses to intensification as well as providing many detailed examples of collaborative research methods.

Contents

Introduction: Adapting to intensification – Resisting through collaboration: A whole-school perspective of the National Curriculum – The creative use and defence of space: Appropriation through the environment – The charisma of the critical other: Enhancing the role of the teacher – Teaching, and researching the teaching of, a history topic: An experiment in collaboration – Managing marginality: Aspects of the career of a primary school head – Self-determination among primary school teachers – References – Index.

208pp   0 335 19313 7 (Paperback)   0 335 19314 5 (Hardback)